Patterns in Java™, Volume 2

Patterns in Java™, Volume 2

MARK GRAND

WILEY COMPUTER PUBLISHING

John Wiley & Sons, Inc.
New York • Chichester • Weinheim • Brisbane • Singapore • Toronto

Publisher: Robert Ipsen
Editor: Theresa Hudson
Assistant Editor: Kathryn A. Malm
Managing Editor: Angela Murphy
Electronic Products, Associate Editor: Mike Sosa
Text Design & Composition: North Market Street Graphics

This book is printed on acid-free paper. ∞

Published by John Wiley & Sons, Inc.

Published simultaneously in Canada.

This publication is designed to provide accurate and authoritative information
in regard to the subject matter covered. It is sold with the understanding that
the publisher is not engaged in professional services. If professional advice or
other expert assistance is required, the services of a competent professional person should be sought.

Library of Congress Cataloging-in-Publication Data:
Grand, Mark.
        Patterns in Java : a catalog of reusable design patterns
illustrated with UML / Mark Grand.
            p.   cm.
        "Wiley computer publishing"
        Includes bibliographical references and index.
            1. Java (Computer program language)   2. UML (Computer science)
3. Software patterns.   I. Title.
QA76.76.P37G73   1998
005. 13'—dc21   98-29976
ISBN 0-471-25839-3 (v. i. : pbk.)
ISBN 0-471-25841-5 (v. ii : pbk.)

Printed in the United States of America.

10 9 8 7 6 5 4 3 2 1

C O N T E N T S

ACKNOWLEDGMENTS

This book would not have been possible without the inspiration, encouragement, and assistance of others. The largest share of that credit goes to my loving wife, Ginni, who is an amazing and wonderful person. Without her constant support, this book would not have been written. She encouraged me to write this and then put up with the long hours I spent writing. I also want to thank my daughters, Rachel and Shana, for their patience.

I want to thank Check Suscheck who provided me with valuable feedback on the GUI Design Patterns chapter.

I want to thank Brad Appleton for his diligent reviews and concern with form.

I want to thank Craig Larman for discovering the GRASP patterns and his feedback on the way the GRASP patterns are presented in this book.

I want to thank Larry O'Brien who provided highly insightful, constructive, and the most easy-to-use feedback. The quality of his feedback reflects his years of editorial experience.

I want to thank the Sydney, Australia, patterns group for their interesting and outspoken critique of some of my chapters.

Finally, I want to thank David Bussee who provided feedback on the Testing Patterns chapter.

ABOUT THE AUTHOR

Mark Grand is a consultant specializing in Java and object-oriented topics with over 20 years of experience. In addition to authoring the *Patterns in Java* series for John Wiley & Sons, he is the author of two Java reference manuals from O'Reilly & Associates and numerous magazine articles. Mark has had a lengthy career as a software developer. In his role as a consultant, Mark has provided mentoring and training in Java and object-oriented techniques to numerous organizations. Mark has been involved in multiple, large-scale commercial Java projects as an architect, mentor, and technical lead. Prior to his involvement with Java, Mark spent over 11 years as a designer and implementor of 4GLs. His most recent role in this vein was as the architect and project manager for an electronic data interchange product. Mark has worked with a number of MIS organizations in such capacities as Oracle database architect, network designer and administrator, and Sun system administrator. He has been involved with object-oriented programming and design since 1982. Mark Grand has a B.S. degree in computer science from Syracuse University. He can be contacted through his Web page, at http://www.mindspring.com/~mgrand.

1

Introduction to Software Patterns

Software patterns are reusable solutions to recurring problems that occur during software development. Because this book is all about software patterns, they are simply referred to as *patterns* for the remainder of this book.

What makes a bright, experienced programmer much more productive than a bright but inexperienced programmer is *experience*. Experience gives programmers a variety of wisdom. As programmers gain experience, they recognize the similarity between new problems and problems they have solved before. With even more experience, they recognize that the solutions for similar problems follow recurring patterns. With the knowledge of these patterns, experienced programmers recognize the situations to which patterns apply and can immediately use the solution without having to stop, analyze the problem, and pose possible strategies.

When a programmer discovers a pattern, it's just an insight. In most cases, it is surprisingly difficult to go from a not-yet-verbalized insight to a well-thought-out idea that the programmer can clearly articulate. It's also an extremely valuable step. When programmers understand a pattern well enough to put it into words, they are able to intelligently combine it with other patterns. More important, once a pattern is put into words, it can be discussed among programmers who know the pattern. This allows programmers to collaborate and combine their wisdom more effectively. It can also help to avoid the situation in which programmers argue over different solutions to a problem, only to find out later that they were really thinking of the same solution but were expressing it in different ways.

Putting a pattern into words has an additional benefit for less experienced programmers. Once a pattern has been put into words, more experienced programmers can teach it to programmers who aren't yet familiar with it.

This book is intended to provide experienced programmers with a common vocabulary to discuss patterns. It will also allow programmers who have not yet discovered some patterns to learn about them.

This book includes a substantial breadth of patterns, but there are still additional patterns that could not be included due to time constraints. Readers may discover some of these patterns. Some of these patterns may be highly specialized and of interest to only a small number of people. Other patterns may be of very broad interest and worthy of inclusion in a revised edition of this book. Readers who wish to communicate such a pattern can drop the author an e-mail at mgrand@mindspring.com.

The patterns cataloged in this book convey constructive ways of organizing parts of the software development cycle. There are other patterns that recur in programs that are not constructive. These types of patterns are called *AntiPatterns*. Because AntiPatterns can cancel out the benefits of patterns, this book does not attempt to catalog them.

A Brief History of Patterns

The idea of software patterns originally came from the field of architecture. Christopher Alexander, an architect, wrote two revolutionary books that describe patterns in building architecture and urban planning: *A Pattern Language: Towns, Buildings, Construction* (Oxford University Press, 1977) and *The Timeless Way of Building* (Oxford University Press, 1979). The ideas presented in these books are applicable to a number of fields outside of architecture, including software.

In 1987, Ward Cunningham and Kent Beck used some of Alexander's ideas to develop five patterns for user-interface (UI) design. They published a paper on the UI patterns at OOPSLA-87 entitled *Using Pattern Languages for Object-Oriented Programs*, by Addison-Wesley [Beck-Cunningham87].

In the early 1990s, Erich Gamma, Richard Helm, Ralph Johnson, and John Vlissides began work on one of the most influential computer books of this decade: *Design Patterns*. The book, published in 1994, popularized the idea of patterns. *Design Patterns* is often called the *Gang of Four* or *GoF* book.

Patterns in Java, Volume 2 represents an evolution of patterns and objects since the GoF book was published. The GoF book used C++ and Smalltalk for its examples. This book uses Java and takes a rather Java-centric view of most things. When the GoF book was written, Unified Modeling Language (UML) did not exist. It is now widely accepted as the preferred notation for object-oriented analysis and design. Therefore, UML is the notation used in this book.

Description of Patterns

Patterns are usually described using a format that includes the following information:

- A description of the problem that includes a concrete example and a solution specific to the concrete problem
- A summary of the forces that lead to the formulation of a general solution
- A general solution
- The consequences, good and bad, of using the given solution to solve a problem
- A list of related patterns

Pattern books differ in how they present this information. The format used in this book varies with the phase of the software life cycle that the pattern addresses. The patterns in this volume are related to a few different phases of the software life cycle. The descriptions of patterns in this volume are organized into sections with the following headings. Because the nature of the patterns vary, not every section heading is used for every pattern.

Pattern Name. The heading of this section consists of the name of the pattern and a bibliography reference that indicates the origin of the pattern. Most patterns don't have any additional text under this heading. For those that do, this section contains information about the derivation or general nature of the pattern.

The bibliography reference indicates where the ideas in the pattern were first written in pattern form. Because patterns are based on established practices, in many cases the ideas in the pattern stem from sources other than the bibliography reference. Usually the author of a pattern is not the first person to discover the ideas that underlie the pattern. I do not claim to be the first person to discover any of the ideas in this book. Patterns for which I am unaware of any other publication that documents that particular set of ideas as a pattern, have a bibliography reference to this book. The bibliography entry next to a pattern name is provided to help you trace the development of the pattern itself, not the underlying ideas.

Synopsis. This section contains a brief description of the pattern. The synopsis conveys the essence of the solution provided by the pattern. The synopsis is primarily directed at experienced programmers who may recognize the pattern as one they already know, but for which they may not have had a name. After recognizing the pattern from its name and synopsis, it may be sufficient to skim the rest of the pattern description.

Don't be discouraged if you don't recognize a pattern from its name and synopsis. Instead, carefully read through the rest of the pattern description to understand it.

Context. This section describes the problem that the pattern addresses. For most patterns, the "Context" section introduces the problem in terms of a concrete example and suggests a design solution.

Forces. This section summarizes the considerations that lead to the problem's general solution, which is presented in the "Solution" section.

Solution. This section is the core of the pattern. It describes a general-purpose solution to the problem that the pattern addresses.

Consequences. This section explains the implications, good and bad, of using the solution.

Implementation. This section describes the important considerations to be aware of when executing the solution. It may also describe some common variations or simplifications of the solution. Some patterns may not have an "Implementation" section because these concerns are not relevant to every pattern.

Java API Usage. When there is an appropriate example of the pattern in the core Java API, it is pointed out in this section. This section is not included for those patterns that are not used in the core Java API.

Code Example. This section contains a code example that shows a sample implementation for a design that uses the pattern. For some patterns, such as GUI design patterns, a code example is not relevant. In some cases, a different sort of example is relevant.

Related Patterns. This section contains a list of patterns that are related to the pattern described.

Organization of This Book

The *Patterns in Java* series of books covers a wider range of patterns than is found in previously published works. Even with the goal of providing coverage of a broad selection of patterns, time constraints have limited the number of patterns that are included. Three volumes of this work are currently planned. If there is sufficient interest, more volumes will follow.

The first volume focuses exclusively on general-purpose design patterns. This second volume includes a variety of patterns used for the following purposes:

- Assigning responsibilities to classes
- Designing GUIs
- Writing code
- Testing software

The third volume will contain design patterns for use in enterprise applications. The planned topics include patterns related to transaction design, distributed computing, and the use of relational databases with object-oriented programs.

Each volume begins with a description of the subset of UML used in that volume. Chapter 3 in each volume contains an overview of the software life cycle, to provide the context in which the patterns are used. Chapter 3 also provides a case study that includes examples for using patterns in that particular volume. The remaining chapters describe different types of patterns.

The CD-ROM that accompanies this volume contains all of the code examples that are found in this book. In some cases, the examples on the CD-ROM are more complete than the examples that appear in this book. The CD-ROM also contains some software related to the patterns in this volume.

The Java examples that appear in this book are based on Java 2. The UML diagrams in this book are based on version 1.1 of the Object Management Group's UML standard.

2

Overview of UML

The *Unified Modeling Language* (UML) is a notation that you can use for object-oriented analysis and design. This chapter contains a brief overview of UML that introduces you to both the subset and extensions to UML used in this book. For a complete description of UML, see http://www.rational.com/uml/documentation.html.

Books that are specifically about UML call the pieces of information stored in instances of a class *attributes;* they call a class's encapsulations of behavior *operations.* Those terms, like UML, are not specific to any implementation language. This book is not language neutral. It assumes that you are using Java as your implementation language. This book also uses Java-specific terms in most places, rather than terms that are language neutral but less familiar to Java programmers. For example, this book uses the words *attribute* and *variable* interchangeably, with preference for the Java-specific term *variable.* This book also uses the words *operation* and *method* interchangeably, with preference for the Java-specific term *method.*

UML defines a number of different kinds of diagrams. The kinds of diagrams found in this book are *class diagrams, collaboration diagrams,* and *statechart diagrams.* The rest of this chapter is organized into sections that describe each of these diagrams and the elements that appear in them.

Class Diagram

A class diagram is a diagram that shows classes, interfaces, and their relationships. The most basic element of a class diagram is a *class.* Figure 2.1 provides an example of a class that shows many of the features that a class can have within a class diagram.

Classes are drawn as rectangles. The rectangles can be divided into two or three compartments. The class rectangle shown in Figure 2.1 has three compartments. The top compartment contains the name of the class. The middle compartment lists the class's variables. The bottom compartment lists the class's methods.

The symbols that precede each variable and method are *visibility indicators.* There are three different types of visibility indicators, as shown in Table 2.1. The variables in the middle compartment are shown as

```
visibilityIndicator name : type
```

Therefore, the two variables shown in the class are private variables. The name of the first variable is `instance` and its type is

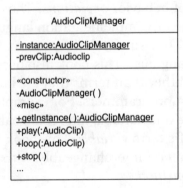

FIGURE 2.1 Basic class.

TABLE 2.1 Visibility Indicators

Visibility Indicators	Meaning
+	Public
#	Protected
−	Private

AudioClipManager. The name of the second variable is `prevClip` and its type is `AudioClip`.

Though not shown in Figure 2.1, an initial value can be indicated for a variable by following the variable's type with an equal (=) sign and the value like this:

```
ShutDown:boolean = false
```

Notice that the first variable shown in the class is underlined. If a variable is underlined that means that it's a static variable. This applies to methods, too. Underlined methods are static methods.

The methods in the bottom compartment are shown as

```
visibilityIndicator name ( formalParameters ) : returnType
```

The `getInstance` method shown in the class found in Figure 2.1 returns an `AudioClipManager` object.

UML indicates a void method by leaving out the "`: return-Type`" from a method to indicate that it doesn't return anything. Therefore, the `stop` method shown in Figure 2.1 does not return any result.

A method's formal parameters consist of a name and a type like this:

```
setLength(length:int)
```

If a method has multiple parameters, commas separate them like this:

```
setPosition(x:int, y:int)
```

Two of the methods in the aforementioned class are preceded by a word in guillemets, like this:

```
«constructor»
```

In a UML drawing, a word in guillemets is called a *stereotype*. A stereotype is used like an adjective to modify what comes after it. The `constructor` stereotype indicates that the methods that follow it are constructors. The `misc` stereotype indicates that the methods that come after it are regular methods. Additional uses for stereotypes are described later in this chapter.

One last element that appears in Figure 2.1 is an ellipsis (. . .). If an ellipsis appears in the bottom compartment of a class, it means that the class has additional methods that the diagram does not show. If an ellipsis appears in the middle compartment of a class, it means that the class has additional variables that the diagram does not show.

Often, it's not necessary or helpful to show as many details of a class as were shown in Figure 2.1. A class can also be drawn with only two compartments, as shown in Figure 2.2.

When a class is drawn with only two compartments, its top compartment contains its name and its bottom compartment shows its methods. If a class is drawn with only two compartments, that just means that its variables are not shown. It does not mean that it has no variables.

The visibility indicators may be omitted from methods and variables. When a method or variable is shown without a visibility indicator, it means there is no indication of the method's or the variable's visibility. It does not imply that the methods or variables are public, protected, or private.

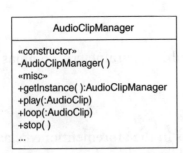

FIGURE 2.2 Two-compartment class.

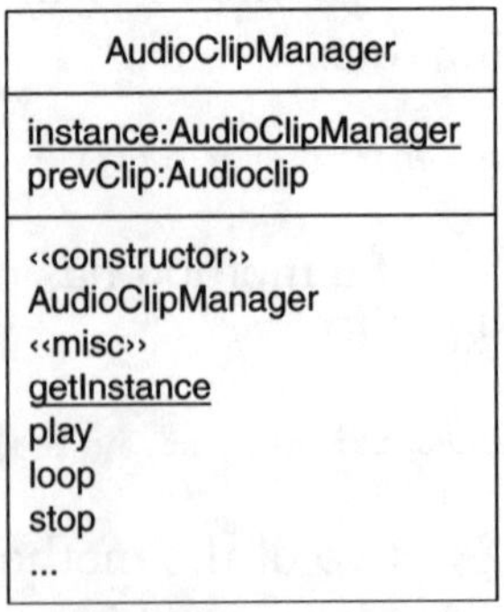

FIGURE 2.3 Simplified class.

AudioClipManager

FIGURE 2.4 One-compartment class.

A method's parameters can be omitted if their return values are also omitted. For example, the visibility indicators and method parameters are omitted from the class shown in Figure 2.3.

Figure 2.4 shows the simplest form of a class, with just one compartment containing the class name. A one-compartment representation of a class merely identifies the class. It provides no indication about the variables or methods that the class has.

Interfaces

Interfaces are drawn in a manner similar to classes. The only difference is that the name in the top compartment is preceded by an «interface» stereotype. Figure 2.5 shows an example of an interface.

Classes and interfaces are important elements of class diagrams. The other elements of a class diagram show the relationships between classes and interfaces. Figure 2.6 is a typical class diagram.

The lines in Figure 2.6 indicate the relationship between the classes and the interface. A solid line with a closed arrowhead like the one in Figure 2.7 indicates the relationship with a subclass that inherits from a superclass. Figure 2.6 shows the

FIGURE 2.5 Interface.

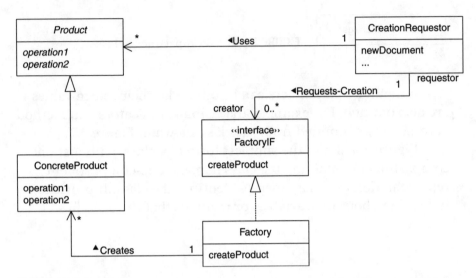

FIGURE 2.6 Class diagram.

abstract class `Product` as the superclass of the `ConcreteProduct` class. You can tell that it's abstract because its name is italicized. You can tell that its methods are abstract because they are also italicized.

A similar sort of line is used to indicate that a class implements an interface. It is represented with a dotted or dashed line with a closed head, like the one shown in Figure 2.8. In Figure 2.6 the `Factory` class implements the `FactoryIF` interface.

The other lines show the other types of relationships between the classes and the interface. UML calls these other types of relationships *associations*. There are a number of things that can appear with an association that provide information about the nature of an association. The following items are optional, but this book consistently uses them wherever it makes sense.

- **Association Name.** Somewhere around the middle of an association there may be an association name. The name of an association is always capitalized. There may be a triangle

FIGURE 2.7 Subclass inherits from superclass.

FIGURE 2.8 Class implements an interface.

at one end of the association name. The triangle suggests the direction in which you read the association. An example of this is found in Figure 2.6, where you see that the association between the `Factory` and `ConcreteProduct` classes has the name `Creates`.

- **Navigation Arrows.**   Arrowheads that appear at the ends of an association are called *navigation arrows*. Navigation arrows indicate the direction in which you can navigate an association. Looking at the association named `Creates` in Figure 2.6, you see that it has a navigation arrow pointing from the `Factory` class to the `ConcreteProduct` class. That means `Factory` objects will have a reference that allows them to access `ConcreteProduct` objects, but not the other way around.

  Because of the nature of creation, it seems clear that this means the Factory class is responsible for creating instances of the ConcreteProduct class. The nature of some associations is less obvious. To clarify the nature of such associations, it may be necessary to supply additional information about the association. One common way to do this is to name the role that each class plays in the association.

- **Role Name.**   To clarify the nature of an association, the name of the role that each class plays in the association can appear at each end of an association, next to the corresponding class. Role names are always lowercase. That makes them easier to distinguish from association names, which are always capitalized. The class diagram shown in Figure 2.6 shows the `CreationRequestor` class and the `FactoryIF` interface participating in an association named `Requests-Creation`. The `CreationRequestor` class participates in that association in a role called `requestor`. The `FactoryIF` interface participates in that association in a role called `creator`.

- **Multiplicity Indicator.**   Another detail of an association that is usually supplied is how many instances of each class participate in an occurrence of an association. A multiplicity indicator may appear at each end of an association to provide that information. A multiplicity indicator can be a simple number like 0 or 1. It can be a range of numbers indicated like this:

`0..2`

An asterisk used as the high value of a range means an unlimited number of occurrences. The multiplicity indicator 1..* means at least one instance; 0..* means any number of instances. A simple * is equivalent to 0..*. Looking at the multiplicity indicators in Figure 2.6, you see that each one of the associations in the drawing is a one-to-many relationship.

Figure 2.9 is a class diagram that shows a class with multiple subclasses.

Figure 2.9 is perfectly valid. However, UML provides a more aesthetically pleasing way to draw a class with multiple subclasses. You can combine the arrowheads, as shown in Figure 2.10. Figure 2.10 is identical in meaning to the diagram shown in Figure 2.9.

Occasionally there is a need to convey more structure than is implied by a simple one-to-many relationship. The type of one-to-many relationship in which one object contains a collection of other objects is called an *aggregation*. A hollow diamond at the end of an association indicates aggregation. The hollow diamond appears at the end of the association attached to the class that contains instances of the other class. The class diagram in Figure 2.11 shows an aggregation.

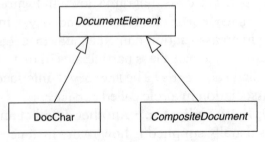

FIGURE 2.9 Multiple inheritance arrows.

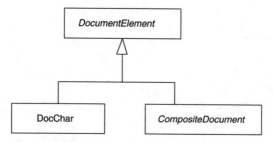

FIGURE 2.10 Single inheritance arrow.

Figure 2.11 shows a class named `MessageManager`. Each of its instances contains zero or more instances of a class named `MIMEMsg`.

UML has another notation that indicates a stronger relationship than aggregation. This relationship is called *composite aggregation*. For an aggregation to be composite:

- Aggregated instances must belong to only one composite at a time.
- Some operations must propagate from the composite to its aggregated instances. For example, when a composite object is cloned, its clone method typically clones the aggregated instances so that the cloned composite owns clones of the original aggregated instances.

Figure 2.12 shows a class diagram that contains composite aggregations.

Figure 2.12 shows a `Document` class. `Document` objects can contain `Paragraph` objects. `Paragraph` objects can contain `DocChar` objects. Because of the composite aggregation, you know that `Paragraph` objects do not share `DocChar` objects and `Document` objects do not share `Paragraph` objects.

Some associations are indirect. Instead of classes that are directly associated with each other, they are associated indirectly

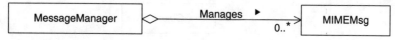

FIGURE 2.11 Aggregation.

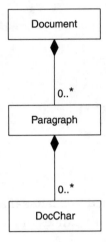

FIGURE 2.12 Composite aggregation.

through a third class. Consider the class diagram shown in Figure 2.13. The association shows that instances of the `Cache` class refer to instances of the `Object` class through an instance of the `ObjectID` class.

There is another use for the ellipsis in a class diagram. Some class diagrams need to show that a class has a large or open-ended set of subclasses, while showing only a few subclasses as examples of the sort of subclasses that the class has. Figure 2.14 shows how an ellipsis can be used to show just that.

The class diagram in Figure 2.14 shows a class named `DataQuery` that has subclasses named `JDBCQuery`, `OracleQuery`, `SybaseQuery`, and an indefinite number of other classes that are indicated by the ellipsis.

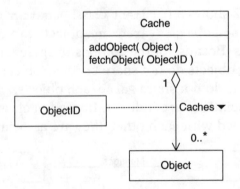

FIGURE 2.13 Association class.

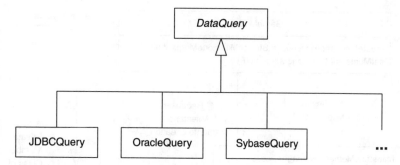

FIGURE 2.14 Open-ended subclasses.

The classes in a class diagram can be organized into *packages*. A package is drawn as a large rectangle with a small rectangle above it. The small rectangle contains the name of the package. The small and large rectangles are arranged with a shape similar to that of a manila folder. The class diagram in Figure 2.15 contains a package named `ServicePackage`.

A visibility indicator can precede the name of a class or interface that appears within a package. Public classes are accessible to classes outside of the package; private classes are not.

Sometimes there are aspects of a design that cannot be made sufficiently clear without a comment in a diagram. A comment in UML is drawn as a rectangle with its upper right corner turned

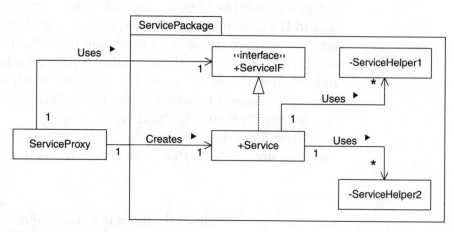

FIGURE 2.15 Package.

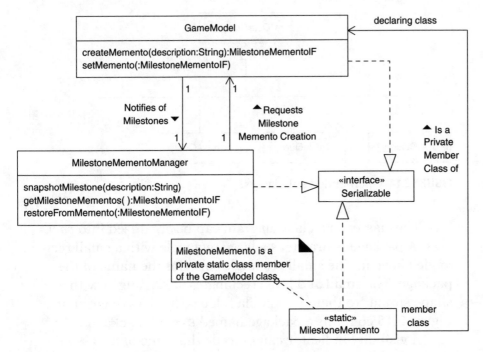

FIGURE 2.16 Private-static classes with a comment.

down. The comment is attached by a dashed line to the diagram element that it relates to. The class diagram in Figure 2.16 contains a comment.

Figure 2.16 shows the static class MilestoneMemento, which is a private member of the GameModel class. There is no standard way in UML to represent a static, private-member class. The diagram uses a stereotype as an extension to UML to indicate that the MilestoneMemento class is static. It uses an association to indicate that the MilestoneMemento is a private member of the GameModel class. To make the relationship even more clear, there is a comment about it in the class diagram.

Class diagrams can include objects. Most of the objects in the diagrams found in this book are drawn as in Figure 2.17.

:Area

FIGURE 2.17 Object in a class diagram.

The object shown in Figure 2.17 is an instance of a class named `Area`. The underline in the object tells you that it's an object. A name may appear to the left of the colon (:). The only significance of the name is that you can use it to identify the individual object.

Some diagrams indicate an object as just an empty rectangle with nothing inside of the rectangle. Obviously, blank objects cannot be used to identify any particular kind of object. However, they can be used in a diagram that shows a structure in which the objects of unspecified type are connected. Figure 2.18 shows such a structure.

The lines that connect two objects are not associations. They are called *links*. Links are connections between objects, whereas associations are relationships between classes. A link is an occurrence of an association, just as an object is an instance of a class. Links can have association names, navigation arrows, and most of the other embellishments that associations can have. However, since a link is a connection between two objects, links may not have multiplicity indicators or aggregation diamonds.

Some diagrams consist of just objects and links. Such diagrams are considered a kind of class diagram. However, there is a special name for diagrams that consist of only objects and links: *object diagram*. Figure 2.19 is an example of an object diagram.

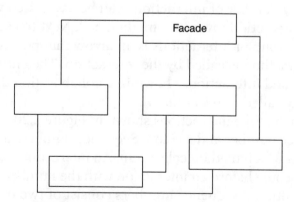

FIGURE 2.18 Blank objects.

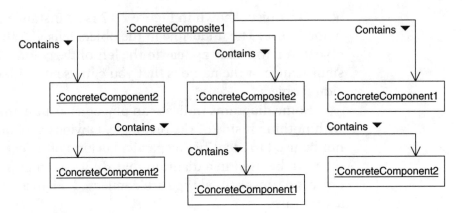

FIGURE 2.19 Object diagram.

Collaboration Diagram

Class and object diagrams show relationships between classes and objects. They also provide information about the interactions that occur between classes. They don't show the sequence in which the interactions occur or any concurrency that they may have.

Collaboration diagrams show objects, the links that connect them, and the interactions that occur over each link. They also show the sequence and concurrency requirements for each interaction. Figure 2.20 is a simple example of a collaboration diagram.

Any number of interactions can be associated with a link. Each interaction involves a method call. Next to each interaction or group of interactions is an arrow that points to the object whose method is called by the interaction. The entire set of objects and interactions shown in a collaboration diagram is collectively called a *collaboration*.

Each of the interactions shown in Figure 2.20 starts with a sequence number and a colon. Sequence numbers indicate the order in which method calls occur. An interaction with the number 1 must come before an interaction with the number 2, and so on.

Multilevel sequence numbers consist of two or more numbers separated by a period. Notice that most of the sequence numbers in Figure 2.20 are multilevel sequence numbers.

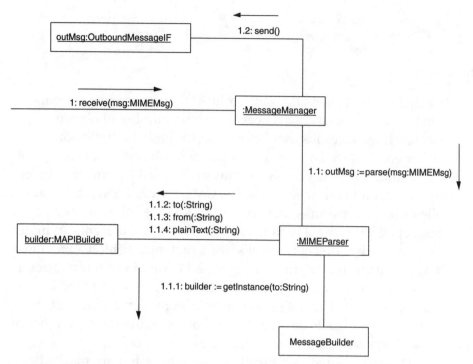

FIGURE 2.20 Collaboration diagram.

Multilevel sequence numbers correspond to multiple levels of method calls. The area of the multilevel sequence number to the left of its rightmost period is called its *prefix*. For example, the prefix of 1.3.4 is 1.3.

Interactions numbered with a multilevel sequence number occur during another interaction's method call. The other method call is determined by the interaction's prefix. So the method calls of the interactions numbered 1.1 and 1.2 are made during the method call of interaction 1. Similarly, interactions numbered 1.1.1, 1.1.2, 1.1.3, and so on, occur during the method call of interaction 1.1.

Among interactions numbered with the same prefix, their methods are called in the order determined by the number following their sequence number prefix. Therefore, the methods of interactions numbered 1.1.1, 1.1.2, 1.1.3, and so on, are called in that order.

As mentioned previously, links represent a connection between two objects. Because of that, links cannot have multiplic-

FIGURE 2.21 Multiobject.

ity indicators. This works well for links that represent an occurrence of an association between a definite number of objects. However, associations that have a star multiplicity indicator on either end involve an indefinite number of objects. For this type of association, there is no way to draw an indefinite number of links to an indefinite number of objects. UML provides a symbol that allows us to draw links that connect to an indefinite number of projects. That symbol is called a *multiobject*. It represents an indefinite number of objects. It looks like a rectangle behind a rectangle. The collaboration diagram in Figure 2.21 contains a multiobject. It shows an `ObservableIF` object calling a `Multicaster` object's `notify` method. The `Multicaster` object's implementation of the `notify` method calls the `notify` method of an indefinite number of `ObserverIF` objects linked to the `Multicaster` object.

Objects created as a result of a collaboration are marked with the property `{new}`. Temporary objects that exist only during a collaboration are marked with the property `{transient}`.* The collaboration diagram in Figure 2.22 shows a collaboration that creates an object.

Some interactions occur concurrently, rather than sequentially. A letter at the end of a sequence number indicates concurrent interactions. For example, the methods of interactions numbered 2.2a and 2.2b are called concurrently and each call runs in a separate thread. Consider the collaboration diagram shown in Figure 2.23. Notice that the top-level interaction is numbered 1. During that interaction, first interaction 1.1 is invoked. Then interactions 1.2a and 1.2b are invoked at the same time. After that, interactions 1.3 and 1.4 are invoked, in that order. An asterisk after a sequence number indicates a repeated interaction, as shown in Figure 2.24.

---

* UML's use of the word *transient* is very different from the way that Java uses it. Java uses *transient* to mean that a variable is not part of an object's persistent state. UML uses it to mean that an object has a bounded lifetime.

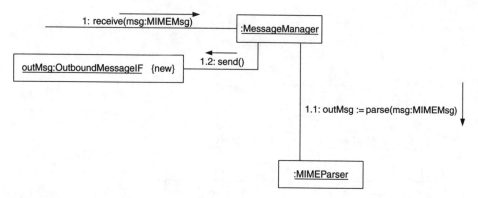

FIGURE 2.22 New object.

The collaboration diagram in Figure 2.24 begins by calling the `TollBooth` object's `start` method. That method repeatedly calls the object's `collectNextToll` method. Each call to the `collectNextToll` method calls the `TollBasket` object's `collectToll` method and the `TollGate` object's `raiseGate` method.

One other thing to notice about this collaboration diagram is the «self» stereotype that appears next to the link for interaction 1.1. This stereotype serves to clarify the fact that the link is a self-reference.

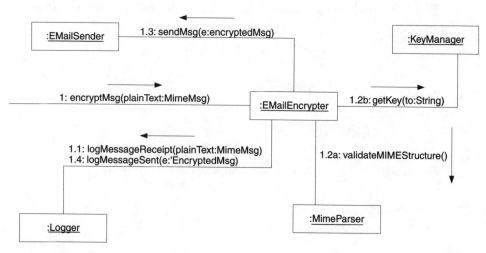

FIGURE 2.23 E-mail encrypter.

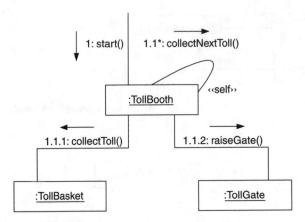

FIGURE 2.24 Tollbooth collaboration diagram.

Unlike the example shown in Figure 2.24, most repetitive interactions occur conditionally. UML allows a condition to be associated with a repetitive interaction by putting it after the asterisk inside of square brackets. Figure 2.25 shows an example of a conditional repetitive interaction where the `Iterator` object is passed to a `DialogMediator` object's `refresh` method. Its `refresh` method, in turn, calls a `Widget` object's `reset` method and then repeatedly calls its `addData` method, while the `Iterator` object's `hasNext` method returns true.

You can indicate that a non-repetitive interaction is conditional, by including a condition without an asterisk in the interaction.

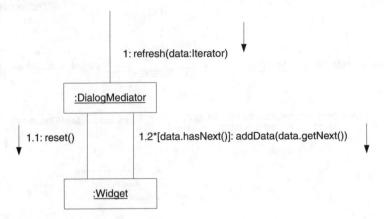

FIGURE 2.25 Refresh.

It's important to note that the definition of UML does not define the meaning of conditions associated with repetitive interactions very precisely. In particular, the definition of UML says that what appears between the square brackets can "be expressed in pseudocode or an actual programming language." This book consistently uses Java for that purpose.

When dealing with multiple threads, something that often requires specification about methods is what happens when two threads try to call the same method at the same time. UML specifies this by placing one of the following constructs after a method:

```
{concurrency = sequential}
```

This means that only one thread at a time calls a method. No guarantee is made about the correctness of the method's behavior if the method is called with multiple threads at a time.

```
{concurrency = concurrent}
```

This means that if multiple threads call a method at the same time, they all execute it concurrently and correctly.

```
{concurrency = guarded}
```

This means that if multiple threads call a method at the same time, only one thread at a time is allowed to execute the method. While one thread executes the method, other threads are forced to wait until it's their turn. This is similar to the behavior of synchronized Java methods. Figure 2.26 shows an example of a synchronized method.

There are refinements to thread synchronization used in this book for which there is no standard representation in UML. This book uses some extensions to the `{concurrency = guarded}` construct to represent those refinements.

In some cases, the object on which threads must synchronize is not the same object whose method is called by an interaction. Consider Figure 2.27. In this collaboration diagram, `{concurrency=guarded:out}` refers to the object labeled `out`. Before the method call can actually take place, the thread that controls the call must own the lock associated with the `out`

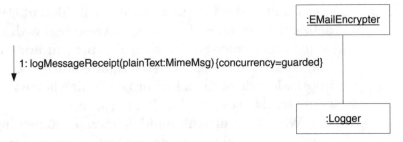

FIGURE 2.26 Synchronized method call.

object. That is identical to Java's semantics for a synchronized statement.

Sometimes there are preconditions beyond acquiring ownership of a lock that must be met before a thread may proceed with a method call. This book represents such preconditions with a vertical bar followed by the precondition. Figure 2.28 shows such preconditions following guarded and a vertical bar.

The collaboration diagram in Figure 2.28 shows two asynchronous interactions. One interaction calls a PrintQueue object's addPrintJob method to add a print job to the PrintQueue object. In the other interaction, a PrintDriver object calls the Print-Queue object's getPrintJob method to get a print job from the PrintQueue object. Both interactions have synchronization preconditions. If the print queue is full, then the interaction that calls the addPrintJob method waits until the print queue is not

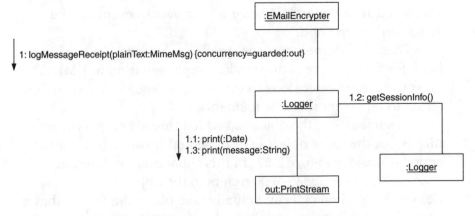

FIGURE 2.27 Synchronization using a third object.

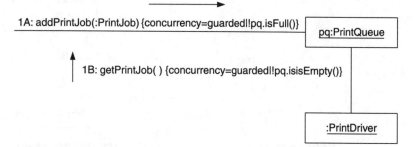

FIGURE 2.28 Print queue.

full before proceeding to make the call to the addPrintJob method. If the print queue is empty, then the interaction that calls the getPrintJob method waits until the print queue is not empty before proceeding to make the call to the getPrintJob method.

These mechanisms determine when the methods of a collaboration are called. They don't say anything about when method calls return. The arrows that point at the objects whose methods are called provide information about when the methods can return.

All the arrows in Figure 2.28 have closed heads, which indicate that the calls are synchronous. The method calls do not return until the method has completed doing whatever it does.

An open arrowhead indicates an asynchronous method call. An asynchronous method call returns to its caller immediately, while the method does its work asynchronously in a separate thread. The collaboration diagram in Figure 2.29 shows an asynchronous method call.

UML defines arrowheads only for synchronous and asynchronous calls. As extensions to UML, UML allows other types of arrows to indicate different types of method calls. To indicate a balking call, this book uses a bent-back arrow, as shown in Figure 2.30.

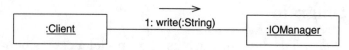

FIGURE 2.29 Asynchronous method call.

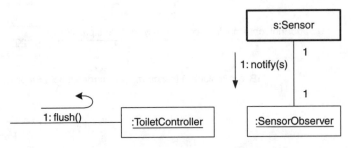

FIGURE 2.30 Balking call depicted with a bent-back arrow.

FIGURE 2.31 Active object `Sensor`.

When a balking call is made to an object's method and there is no other thread executing that object's method, the method returns when it is finished doing what it does. However, when a balking call is made and there is another thread currently executing that object's method, the method returns immediately without performing anything.

You may have noticed that the object that makes the top-level call that initiates a collaboration is not shown in all of the collaboration diagrams. This means that the object that initiates the collaboration is not considered to be a part of the collaboration.

The objects in UML that you have seen up to this point are passive in nature. They don't do anything until one of their methods is called.

Some objects are active. They have a thread associated with them that allows them to initiate operations asynchronously and independently of whatever else is going on in a program. An *active object* is indicated as an object with a thick border. Figure 2.31 contains an example of an active object.

In the diagram an active `Sensor` object calls a `SensorObserver` object's method without another object first calling one of its methods.

Statechart Diagram

Statechart diagrams are used to model a class's behavior as a state machine. Figure 2.32 is an example of a simple state diagram.

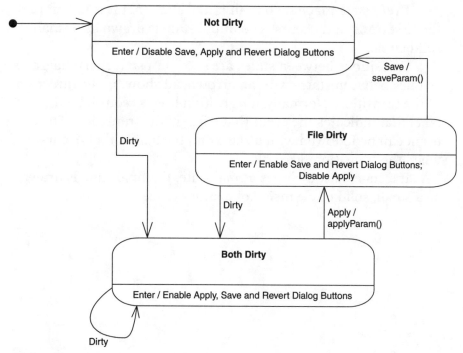

FIGURE 2.32 Statechart diagram.

A statechart diagram shows each state as a rounded rect-angle. All of the states shown in Figure 2.32 are divided into two compartments. The upper compartment contains the name of the state. The lower compartment contains a list of events to which the object responds while in that state, without changing state. Each event in the list is followed by a slash and the action it performs in response to the event. UML predefines two such events:

1. The enter event occurs when an object enters a state.
2. The exit event occurs when an object leaves a state.

If there are no events to which a state responds without changing state, then its rectangle is not divided into two compart-ments. Such a state is drawn as a simple, rounded rectangle that contains only the state's name.

Every state machine has an initial state that it is in before the first transition occurs. The initial state is drawn as a small, solid circle.

Transitions between states are shown in statechart diagrams as lines between states with an arrowhead showing the direction of the transition. Normally, a transition line is required to have a label that indicates the event that triggers the transition. The event can be followed with a slash and the action that occurs when the transition takes place.

If a statechart includes a final state, the final state is drawn as a small, solid circle inside of a larger circle.

The Software Life Cycle

This chapter first describes the software life cycle, then presents the object-oriented design portion of a case study.

A variety of activities take place during the lifetime of a piece of software. Figure 3.1 shows some of the activities that lead up to the deployment of a piece of business software.

This figure is not intended to show all of the activities that take place during a software project. It merely shows some of the common activities for the purpose of understanding the context in which the patterns discussed in this book are used. The three volumes of this work describe recurring patterns that occur during the portion of the software life cycle labeled "Build" in Figure 3.1.

Figure 3.1 shows very clear boundaries between each activity. In practice, the boundaries are not always so discernible. Sometimes it is difficult to determine if a particular activity belongs in one box or another. The precise boundaries are not important. What is important is to understand the relationships between these activities.

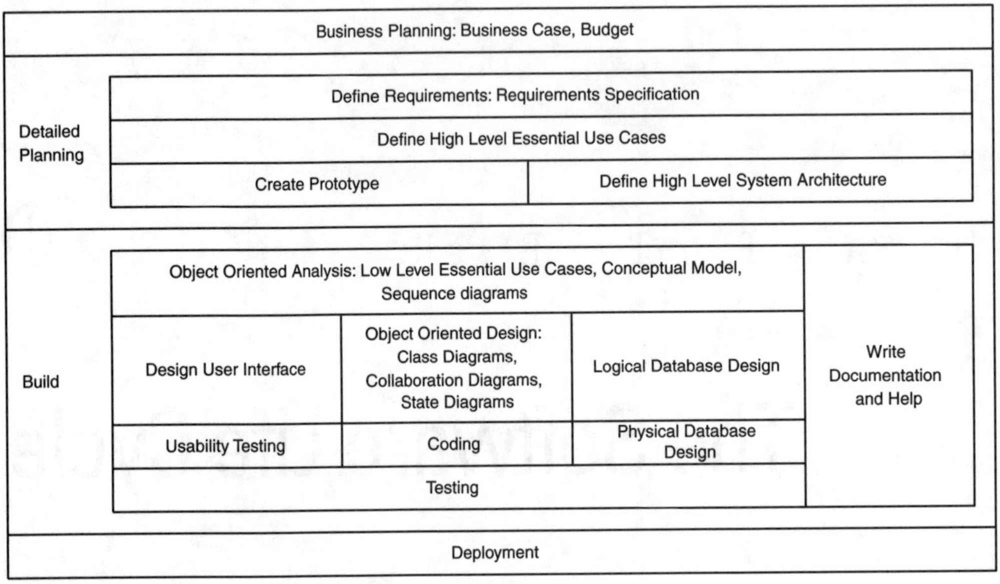

Business Planning: Business Case, Budget
Detailed Planning
Define Requirements: Requirements Specification
Define High Level Essential Use Cases
Create Prototype
Define High Level System Architecture
Build
Object Oriented Analysis: Low Level Essential Use Cases, Conceptual Model, Sequence diagrams
Design User Interface
Object Oriented Design: Class Diagrams, Collaboration Diagrams, State Diagrams
Logical Database Design
Write Documentation and Help
Usability Testing
Coding
Physical Database Design
Testing
Deployment

FIGURE 3.1 Activities that lead to software deployment.

Earlier activities, such as defining requirements and object-oriented analysis, determine the course of the activities that follow them, such as defining essential use cases or object-oriented design. However, in the course of those later activities, deficiencies in the products from earlier activities can emerge. For example, in the course of defining a use case, it may become apparent that there is an ambiguous or conflicting requirement. Making the necessary changes to the requirements generally results in the need to modify existing use cases or write new ones. You should expect such iterations. As long as the trend is for later iterations to produce fewer changes than earlier ones, consider such iterations part of the normal development process.

The following paragraphs are brief descriptions of some of the activities shown in Figure 3.1. The purpose of these descriptions is to provide enough background information about these activities to understand how the patterns discussed in this book apply to a relevant activity. The case study that follows the descriptions provides deeper insights into these activities.

Business Planning   This typically starts with a proposal to build or modify a piece of software. The proposal evolves into a *business case*. A business case is a document that describes the pros and cons of the software project and also includes estimates of the resources required to complete the project. If a decision is made to proceed with the project, a preliminary schedule and budget are prepared.

Define Requirements   The purpose of this activity is to produce a *requirements specification* that indicates what the software produced by the project will and will not do. This typically begins with goals and high-level requirements from the business case. Additional requirements are obtained from appropriate sources to produce an initial requirements specification. As the requirements specification is used in subsequent activities, necessary refinements to the requirements are discovered. These refinements are incorporated into the requirements specification. The products of subsequent activities are then modified to reflect the changes to the requirements specification.

Define Essential Use Cases   A *use case* describes the sequence of events that occurs in a specific circumstance between a system and other entities. The other entities are called *actors*. Developing use cases improves programmers' understanding of the requirements, analysis, or design that the use case is based on. As programmers develop better understanding of requirements, analysis, and design, they are able to refine them.

   Essential use cases describe events in terms of the problem domain. Use cases that describe events in terms of the internal organization of software are called *real use cases*.

   The type of use case most appropriate for refining requirements is the *high-level essential use case*. Such use cases are high level in the sense that they explore the implications of what they are based on, but do not try to add additional details.

Create Prototype   The purpose of this activity is to create a prototype for the proposed software. Programmers can use a prototype to get reactions to a proposed project. Programmers can use reactions to a prototype to refine requirements and essential use cases.

Define High-Level System Architecture The purpose of this activity is to determine the major components of the system that are obvious from the original proposal and their relationships.

Object-Oriented Analysis *Object-oriented analysis* is an analysis of the problem domain. The purpose of this activity is to understand what the software produced by the project will do and how it will interact with other entities in its environment. The goal of analysis is to create a model of what the software will do, but not of how to do it. The products of object-oriented analysis model the situation in which the software will operate, from the perspective of an outside observer. The analysis does not concern itself with what goes on inside the software.

Design User Interface The purpose of this activity is to determine the nature of the interactions between the program and the user based on use cases. Once the nature of the interactions is identified, the user interface is designed and the details of how the user will interact with it are identified.

Object-Oriented Design The purpose of this activity is to determine the internal organization and logic of the software. The products of the design effort identify the classes that constitute the internal logic of the software. They also determine the internal structure of the classes and their interrelationships.

More decisions are made during object-oriented design than during any other activity. For this reason, the three volumes of this work include more patterns that apply to object-oriented design than to any other activity.

Coding The purpose of this activity is to write the code that makes the software work.

Testing The purpose of this phase is to ensure that the software performs as expected.

Case Study

The following case study involves the design and development of an employee timekeeping system for a fictitious business called Henry's Food Market. To keep the size of this example reasonable, the artifacts of the development process are simplified and abbreviated. The details of deriving those artifacts are also abbreviated. The point of this case study is to illustrate the use of the different types of patterns that are covered in this volume.

Business Case

Here is an abbreviated business case that lays out the motivation and schedule for building an employee timekeeping system.

Henry's Food Market operates five retail stores. To support these stores, it also operates a warehouse and a commercial bakery that produces the baked goods that the stores sell. Most of its employees are paid by the hour. A time clock system tracks employee hours. When employees begin work, go on break, return from a break, or leave work, they are supposed to slide their employee badges through a timekeeping clock that records their hours.

Henry's Food Market wants to expand, increasing the number of its stores from 5 to 21 over the next 2 years at a rate of 2 stores every 3 months. One of the challenges the company faces is that if it continues to use the existing timekeeping system, it will have to hire more people to handle the administrative side of timekeeping. Currently, each location requires a person working half-time as a timekeeper to administer its timekeeping system. The activities the timekeeper is required to perform are as follows:

- The timekeeper prints reports for supervisors that show the number of hours each employee worked the previous day. This allows supervisors to verify that their subordinates worked the stated number of hours. Some common errors that are uncovered by supervisors who review these reports are:

    - Employees do not clock out when they go on break or leave work.
    - Coworkers clock in employees who are late for work.
    - Employees clock in before the start of their shift.

- The timekeeper enters corrections into the timekeeping system.
- The timekeeper prepares weekly reports that show the number of hours every employee in a location worked and sends those reports to the payroll department.

The timekeeping system only provides employee hours in the form of a printed report. There is currently one person working full-time to enter employee hours into the payroll system and review the entered hours. This person costs the company $24,000 a year. If the company continues to use this system, it will have to hire an additional person to enter employee hours at an additional cost of $24,000 a year.

The cost of having a person working half-time as a timekeeper in each location is $9,000 per person per year. The current cost of paying people to be timekeepers is $63,000 per year.

The total current cost of labor for timekeeping is $87,000 per year. In two years, when the company's expansion is complete, that labor cost will have increased to $237,000.

The proposed project is to build a replacement timekeeping system that will keep the labor cost of timekeeping at current or lower levels after the expansion. The timekeeping system will be expected to pay for itself in 18 months. Deployment of the system is expected within six months of the start of the project.

Define Requirements Specification

Minimally, a requirements specification should specify the required functions and attributes of what is produced by a project. *Required functions* are things that the system must do, such as record the time that an employee starts work. *Required attributes* are characteristics of the system that are not functions—for example, requiring that the use of the timekeeping terminals not require more than an eighth-grade education. Some other things that are normally found in a requirements document, but are not in the following example, are:

Assumptions This is a list of things that are assumed to be true, such as the minimum educational requirement for employees or the fact that the company will not become unionized.

Risks This is a list of things that can go wrong, leading to delay or failure of the project. This list can include technical uncertainties, such as the availability of devices that are suitable for use as timekeeping terminals. It also can include nontechnical concerns, such as anticipated changes to labor laws.

Dependencies This is a list of resources that this project can depend on, such as the existence of a wide-area network.

It's helpful to number the requirements in a requirements specification. This allows decisions based on a requirement to be easily noted in use cases, design documents, and even code. If inconsistencies are found later on, it is easy to trace them back to the relevant requirements. It is also common to number requirements hierarchically by functions. Here are some of the required functions for the timekeeping system:

R1 The system must collect the times that employees start work, go on break, return from break, and leave work.

    R1.1 In order to work with the timekeeping terminal, employees are required to identify themselves by sliding their employee badges through a badge reader on the timekeeping terminal.

    R1.2 After an employee is identified by a timekeeping terminal, the employee can press a button to indicate if he or she is starting a work shift, going on break, returning from break, or ending a work shift. The timekeeping system keeps a permanent record for each such event in a form that it can later incorporate into a report documenting the employee's hours.

R2 Supervisors must be able to review the hours of subordinates at a timekeeping terminal without any need to get a hard copy.

    R2.1 The timekeeping terminal presents options to supervisors that allow supervisors to review and modify an employee's recorded hours.

> **R2.1.1** All revisions to an employee's timekeeping record leave an audit trail that retains the original records and identifies the person who made each revision.

> **R2.2** To ensure the simplest possible user interface for nonsupervisors, nonsupervisors do not see any options related to supervisory functions when they use a timekeeping terminal.

> **R2.3** Supervisors can modify the timekeeping records only of their own subordinates.

> **R3** At the end of each pay period, the timekeeping system must automatically transmit employee hours to the payroll system.

As we develop some use cases, you can expect to discover additional required functions.

Develop High-Level Essential Use Cases

When developing use cases, it is usually best to focus first on the most common cases and then develop use cases for the less common cases. Use cases for common situations are called *primary use cases*. Use cases for less common situations are called *secondary use cases*. Here is a use case for the most common use of the timekeeping system:

Use case:	Employee Uses Timekeeping Terminal, version 1.
Actor:	Employee.
Purpose:	Inform timekeeping system of an employee's comings and goings.
Synopsis:	An employee is about to begin a work shift, go on break, return from break, or end a work shift. The employee identifies him- or herself to the timekeeping system and lets it know which of those four things he or she is about to do.

Type:	Primary and essential.
Cross References:	Requirements R1, R1.1, R1.2, R1.3, and R2.2.

Course of Events

Employee	System
1. Employee slides his or her badge through a timekeeping terminal's badge reader.	2. The timekeeping terminal reads the employee ID from the badge and verifies that it is a legitimate employee ID. The timekeeping terminal then prompts the employee to tell it if he or she is starting a work shift, going on break, returning from break, or ending a work shift.
3. The employee indicates to the timekeeping terminal whether he or she is starting a work shift, going on break, returning from break, or ending a work shift.	4. The timekeeping terminal makes a permanent record of the employee's indication. It then acknowledges the employee by displaying the current time, indicating that it is ready for use by the next employee.

Now let's consider a larger use case that contains less detail.

Use case:	Employee Uses Multiple Timekeeping Terminals to Track Hours, version 1.
Actor:	Employee.
Purpose:	Inform timekeeping system of an employee's comings and goings during an entire shift.
Synopsis:	An employee who is not restricted to the use of a single timekeeping terminal notifies the timekeeping system when he or she starts a shift, goes on break, returns from break, or ends a shift.
Type:	Primary and essential.
Cross References:	Requirements R1 and R1.2.

Course of Events

Employee	*System*
1. An employee uses a timekeeping terminal to notify the timekeeping system that he or she is starting a shift.	2. The system makes a record of the time that the employee begins the shift.
3. An employee uses a timekeeping terminal to notify the timekeeping system that he or she is going on break.	4. The system makes a record of the time that the employee goes on break.
5. An employee uses a timekeeping terminal to notify the timekeeping system that he or she has returned from break.	6. The system makes a record of the time that the employee returns from break.
7. An employee uses a timekeeping terminal to notify the timekeeping system that he or she is ending a shift.	8. The system makes a record of the time that the employee ends the shift.

When we analyze the less detailed use case, we find a potential problem. There is no requirement that all the timekeeping terminals keep the correct time. Employees are likely to notice if the time on different timekeeping terminals is not the same. They will want to start their shift on the terminal that shows the earlier time and end their shift on the terminal that shows the later time. To prevent employees from cheating the company in this way, we need to add another requirement:

R1.3 The times displayed and recorded by different timekeeping terminals must be within five seconds of each other.

As we develop additional essential use cases, additional refinements to the requirements will be found. However, this is all that we present in the present case study.

Object-Oriented Analysis

Object-oriented analysis is concerned with building a model of the problem that must be solved. It answers the question of what the software will do without concern for how it will do it.

The primary product of object-oriented analysis is a conceptual model of the problem that shows the proposed system and the real-world entities with which the system interacts. The conceptual model also includes the relationships and interactions between the problem domain entities and between the entities and the system.

Conceptual models are usually constructed in two phases:

1. Identify the entities that are involved in the problem. It is very important to identify all of the entities involved. When in doubt, it is best to include an entity in the model. If the entity is unnecessary for subsequent design activities, that fact will become apparent as the design develops. On the other hand, if an entity is missing from the analysis, the missing entity may not be detected later in the project.
2. Identify the relationships between the entities.

UML uses the same symbols to represent the entities and relationships of a conceptual model that it uses to represent classes and associations in a class model. Figure 3.2 is a diagram that shows just the entities that are apparent from the requirements and the use cases. The entities in this figure are in no particular order. The diagram adds some of the more obvious relationships.

When you examine Figure 3.3, notice two entities that are not involved in any of the indicated relationships: `Timekeeping-System` and `EmployeeID`. This diagram is supposed to be a conceptual model of the problem to be solved. Because the `Time-keepingSystem` entity does not seem to have a relationship to anything else in the problem, we conclude that it is really part of the solution rather than the problem. For that reason, we drop it from the model.

The `EmployeeID` entity is very closely related to the `Employee` entity. In fact, it is so closely related to the `Employee` entity that it seems more appropriate to represent it as an attribute. Figure 3.4 shows the conceptual model with attributes added.

The diagram in Figure 3.4 is as far as we take the analysis of this problem.

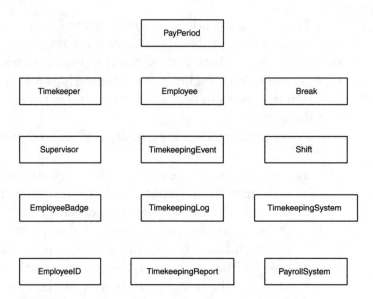

FIGURE 3.2 Conceptual model with entities only.

User Interface Design

User interface design is concerned with the details of how a user interacts with a system. The central concerns are how the system appears to users and what procedures users need to follow when interacting with the system.

The requirements for the employee timekeeping system simplify the design process by requiring each employee interaction to begin with the employee sliding his or her ID card through a card reader. The use cases provide guidance for organizing the rest of the user interface.

One use case states that after the employee slides his or her badge through the card reader, the timekeeping terminal asks the employee to indicate which one of four possible actions the employee is taking. The Menu Interaction pattern indicates that a menu style of interaction is appropriate when you want a user to choose from a limited set of alternatives. The pattern also states that a set of pushbuttons is an appropriate way to present the choices when the choice is the main focus of the interaction and the number of choices is small. This results in the design shown in Figure 3.5.

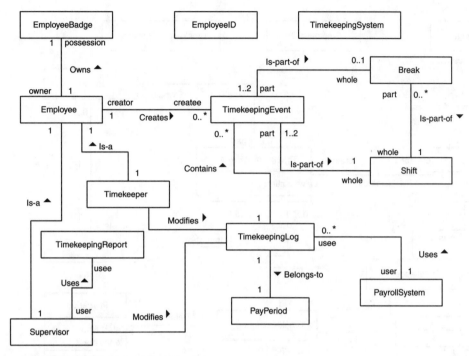

FIGURE 3.3 Conceptual model with associations.

Object-Oriented Design

Object-oriented design is concerned with designing the internal logic of a program—in this case, we are concerned with the internal logic of the timekeeping system. The object-oriented design is not concerned with how the user interface presents that logic, nor is it concerned with how data is stored in a database. The ultimate goal of object-oriented design is to provide a detailed design of the classes that will provide that internal logic.

There are various strategies for using the results of analysis to produce a design. The strategy that we use here is to create a class diagram that models the structural relationships in the conceptual model. We then develop collaboration diagrams to model the behavioral relationships in the conceptual model. After that, we refine the class diagrams with what we learned from the collaboration diagrams. Finally, we refine the collaboration and class diagrams with requirements that are not covered by the

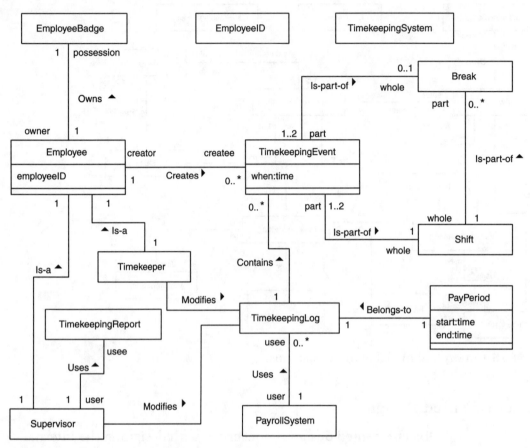

FIGURE 3.4 Conceptual model with attributes.

conceptual model. Throughout that process, we use patterns to guide us.

Let's construct our first class diagram by assuming that there is a class to represent each entity in the conceptual model, as shown in Figure 3.6. Rather than assume the representation of the entity attributes in the conceptual model, the class diagram in this figure indicates accessor methods for the attributes.

Next we need to consider the "Is-a" relationships in the conceptual model. Though an obvious way to represent "Is-a" relationships in a class diagram is through inheritance, the Delegation pattern (described in Volume 1) tells us that that is not always the best way to represent "Is-a" relationships. In par-

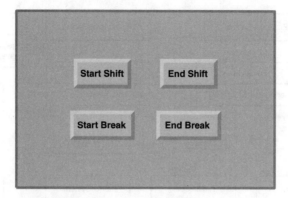

FIGURE 3.5 Timekeeping screen.

ticular, it tells us to use delegation instead of inheritance to depict "Is-a" relationships that represent roles that instances of a class play at different times. Since nonsupervisory employees may be promoted to supervisors, be transferred from another job to the timekeeper job, or become timekeeping supervisors, we use delegation to represent those roles (see Figure 3.7).

The "Is-part-of" relationships in the conceptual diagram are another structural relationship that we can consider designing into the class diagram at this point. Notice that there is some

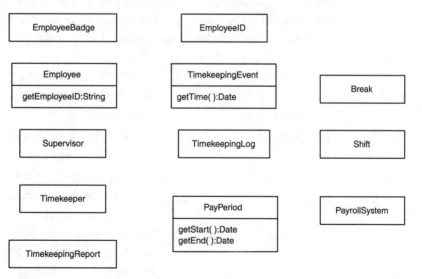

FIGURE 3.6 Class diagram, version 1.

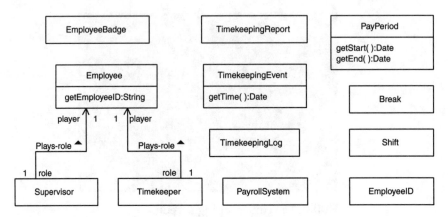

FIGURE 3.7 Class diagram, version 2.

redundancy between two sets of "Is-part-of" relationships: The "Is-part-of" relationship between `Shift` and `TimekeepingEvent` appears to have some redundancy with the set of "Is-part-of" relationships between `Shift` and `Break` and between `Break` and `TimekeepingEvent`. For this reason, we postpone including those relationships in the design until we have clarified the relationships through the construction of collaboration diagrams.

Next we need to assign responsibilities to classes. We guide the construction of collaboration diagrams with use cases, so we assemble the following real use case to describe a typical employee's use of the timekeeping system for one day.

Use case:	Employee Uses Timekeeping Terminal to Track Hours, version 1.
Actor:	Employee.
Purpose:	Inform timekeeping system of an employee's comings and goings.
Synopsis:	An employee is about to start a work shift, go on break, return from break, or end a work shift. The employee identifies him- or herself to the timekeeping system and lets it know which of those four things he or she is about to do.

Type:	Primary and real.
Cross References:	Requirements R1, R1.1, R1.2, R1.3, and R2.2.
Essential use case:	Employee Uses Timekeeping Terminal

Course of Events

Employee	System
1. Employee slides his or her badge through a timekeeping terminal's badge reader.	2. The timekeeping display replaces its display of the current time—indicating that it is available for use—with a display that tells the employee that it is looking up the employee ID detected by the badge reader. After the timekeeping terminal has found the employee's information, it verifies that the employee is allowed to use this particular timekeeping terminal. The timekeeping terminal then prompts the employee to tell it if he or she is starting a work shift, going on break, returning from break, or ending a work shift.
3. The employee indicates to the timekeeping terminal whether he or she is starting a work shift, going on break, returning from break, or ending a work shift.	4. The timekeeping terminal makes a permanent record of the employee's choice. It acknowledges the completion of the timekeeping transaction by displaying the current time, indicating that it is ready for use by the next employee.

This use case involves classes that are not in the previous class diagram. The use case talks about a timekeeping terminal that interacts with a user, so we need to include a user interface class in our design. We may refine that into additional classes if deemed necessary later on.

Next we assign classes responsibility for the actions described in the use case. The collaboration diagram in Figure 3.8 shows those assignments. Here is a description of the interactions found in this collaboration diagram:

1. The use case begins when user slides his or her badge through the badge reader in the timekeeping terminal and

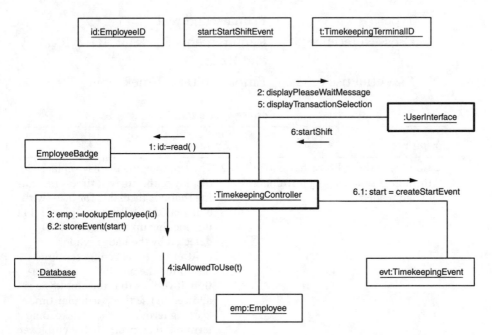

FIGURE 3.8 Start shift collaboration.

the terminal responds. From the timekeeping terminal's point of view, the use case begins when the terminal reads the employee's badge. The class diagram in Figure 3.7 has an `EmployeeBadge` class to which we can reasonably assign the responsibility of reading physical badges. Figure 3.7 does not contain any class that would be an obvious class to call the `EmployeeBadge` class's read method.

The Controller GRASP pattern tells us that external and system events should be received by a controller object rather than the internal objects that will actually handle the events. Based on that guidance, we add a `Time-keepingController` class to our design and make it responsible for calling the `EmployeeBadge` class's read method.

2. The user interface is supposed to display a message that asks the user to wait while the timekeeping terminal validates the employee ID read from the badge. It seems obvious that the `UserInterface` object will be responsible for

displaying messages. We need to assign an object the responsibility of telling the UserInterface object to display the message. The Expert GRASP pattern tells us to assign responsibilities to classes that have the information required to carry out the responsibility. Since the TimekeepingController object already knows a badge has been read, we make it responsible for telling the user interface to display the message.

3. Next, the timekeeping terminal is supposed to get the employee information that corresponds to the employee ID that it read. Since the database is where the employee information resides, we have the TimekeepingController object retrieve information about the employee associated with the employee ID by passing the employee ID to the Database object's LookupEmployee method. The Lookup-Employee method returns an Employee object that encapsulates information about the employee.

4. Because the Employee object contains the employee's information, we give it the responsibility of determining if the employee is supposed to be using this particular timekeeping terminal. We have the TimekeepingController object call the Employee object's isAllowedToUse method.

5. The TimekeepingController object calls the UserInterface object's displayTransactionSelection method. This causes the user interface to prompt the employee for the type of event (starting a shift, starting a break, ending a break, or ending a shift) to record.

6. When the user specifies whether he or she is starting a shift, the UserInterface object calls the Timekeeping-Controller object's startShift method. We give the TimekeepingController object this responsibility because it has the general responsibility of receiving and dispatching external events.

    6.1 The TimekeepingController object creates a TimekeepingEvent object to represent the start-of-shift event. We give the TimekeepingController object this responsibility because the Creator GRASP pattern tells us that if an object has the data required by another object's constructor, this is a reason to give the object responsibility for the other object's creation.

6.2 The `TimekeepingController` object passes the event object to the `Database` object's `storeEvent` method so it can be stored in the database.

This is as far as we take this case study. Hopefully, it has provided you with some insight into how to use some of the different types of patterns presented in this book.

4

GRASP Patterns

General Responsibility Assignment Software Patterns (GRASPs)
present fundamental and universal object-oriented design principles in the form of patterns. GRASP patterns provide direction
for assigning responsibilities to classes and, to a limited extent,
determining the classes that will be in a design.

GRASP patterns were first documented by Craig Larman
[Larman98]. His motivation for formulating this set of patterns

was to help people learn object-oriented design. They can be applied in many other situations, as well.

GRASP patterns are *not* design patterns. They have a fundamentally different flavor. Design patterns provide guidance in solving specific design problems. GRASP patterns provide instruction for assigning responsibilities to classes in a way that results in well-structured designs that are easy to understand and maintain. GRASP patterns are generally used to lead the designer to a situation where a design pattern is applicable. The case study in Chapter 3 provides some examples of the use of GRASP patterns.

This chapter discusses GRASP patterns as they are applied to object-oriented design. However, most GRASP patterns apply equally well to business process reengineering (BPR). GRASP patterns can also be applied to many other types of design efforts in which it is important that the design be easily understood and able to be modified with minimal difficulty.

The first pattern described in this chapter, *Low Coupling/ High Cohesion,* is an important pattern because it shows when to use or revisit other GRASP patterns. The remaining GRASP patterns provide specific guidance on how to assign responsibilities to classes. The two most important of these are the *Expert* and *Polymorphism* GRASP patterns.

Low Coupling/High Cohesion [Larman98]

Low Coupling and High Cohesion were originally published as separate patterns. Because the two are closely related, they are presented here as one unified pattern.

SYNOPSIS

If a class is so highly coupled or lacking in cohesion as to make a design brittle or difficult to modify, then apply other appropriate GRASP patterns to reassign the class's responsibilities.

CONTEXT

Suppose you have the task of designing a system that bills customers for services based on the amount of time that the customer uses them. Figure 4.1 shows the conceptual model on which you will base your design.

In this model, a customer signs up to use one or more services. A `UsageRecord` records the amount of time that the cus-

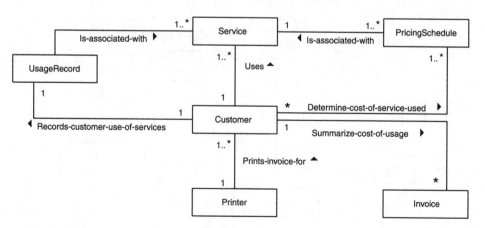

FIGURE 4.1 Service billing conceptual model.

tomer actually uses the services. A `PricingSchedule` is associated with each `Service` that a customer uses. The `PricingSchedule` determines what the customer pays for the associated service. A customer's `UsageRecord` and `PricingSchedule` are combined to create an `Invoice`. Once a `Customer` has an `Invoice`, the `Customer` sends it to a printer.

Creating classes that directly correspond to entities in a conceptual model provides a reasonable first pass at a design. The collaboration diagram in Figure 4.2 shows objects and operations that correspond directly to the conceptual model.

Figure 4.3 shows the class diagram that is implied by the collaboration diagram. When you examine this diagram, notice that there is a problem with the `Customer` class. The requirements for the billing program require it to handle different kinds of customers. The billing program is also required to generate different kinds of invoices, based on the types of services used by the customer and additional considerations other than the type of customer. As it stands, the design is not flexible enough to meet your needs.

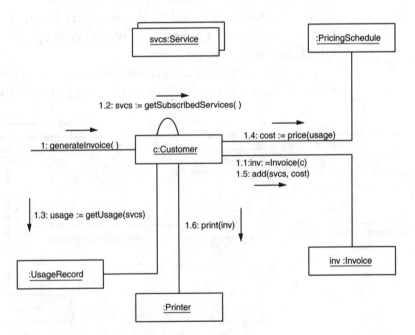

FIGURE 4.2 Service billing collaboration.

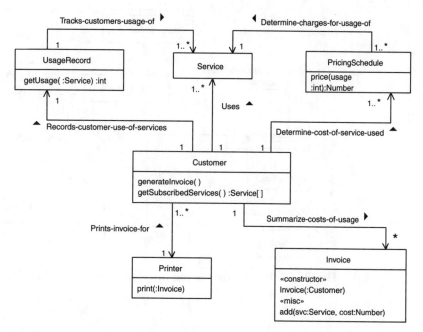

FIGURE 4.3 Service billing classes.

Looking at it from the viewpoint of coupling and cohesion, you notice that the `Customer` class is responsible for determining what services a customer is entitled to use and creating an invoice for the use of those services. Since these are unrelated activities, the `Customer` class is not very cohesive. You also notice that the `Customer` class is more highly coupled to other classes than are the other classes in your design.

The Low Coupling/High Cohesion pattern says that when a design is brittle due to classes having high coupling or low cohesion, you can fix the problem by applying other GRASP patterns.

You can reduce the number of classes to which the `Customer` class is coupled to by using the Pure Fabrication pattern to add the `InvoiceManager` class. This class takes responsibility for generating invoices, as shown in Figure 4.4. Assigning this responsibility to `InvoiceManager` also makes the `Customer` class more cohesive by limiting its responsibility to determining what services a customer is entitled to use.

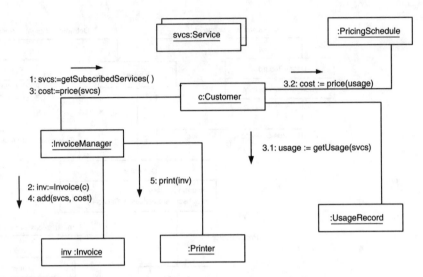

FIGURE 4.4 Pure Fabrication applied to service billing.

FORCES

- Classes that are highly coupled to other classes are difficult to maintain because they are harder to understand in isolation. Classes that lack cohesion are difficult to maintain because they tend to introduce internal dependencies between unrelated functions that are difficult to understand.
- Highly coupled classes are difficult to reuse because they must be used with the classes on which they depend.
- Highly coupled classes require additional maintenance effort because the more classes that a class depends on, the more likely it is that a change to another class will also require a change to the highly coupled class. Conversely, changes to a class with low coupling affect fewer classes, and there are fewer classes that can be affected if the classes are changed.
- It requires more effort to understand a class that is not cohesive than a highly cohesive class. To understand a class that is not cohesive, it is necessary to understand different and possibly unrelated ideas. To understand a cohesive class, it is necessary to understand similar and related ideas.

The other patterns in this chapter show how to assign responsibilities to classes in ways that usually result in designs with low coupling and high cohesion.

SOLUTION

If you find that you are working with a design that is too inflexible or difficult to maintain, look for classes that are highly coupled or that lack cohesion as a possible cause of the problem. A common design problem is that too many responsibilities are assigned to a class, making the class difficult to implement and maintain. These classes are easily recognized because they are highly coupled to other classes or have a set of methods that lack cohesion. Classes that are highly coupled usually lack cohesion and vice versa.

If you find such classes, reorganize them so that the classes in your design have low coupling and high cohesion. You can usually achieve a suitable reorganization by applying other patterns presented in this chapter.

CONSEQUENCES

- Application of this pattern results in classes that have high cohesion and low coupling and that are easier to maintain and reuse.
- Coupling and cohesion are both qualitative measurements. There is no set amount of coupling that is considered too high. Determining what is "too high" is an exercise in judgment. If one class in a design is significantly more coupled to other classes than other classes in the design, then it is probably too highly coupled. If you intend a class to have a high level of reuse, it should have a particularly low level of coupling.
- Excessive coupling and lack of cohesion are common but not the only causes of inflexible and hard-to-maintain designs. Sometimes, the time spent looking for highly coupled classes that lack cohesion is wasted, because the problems have other causes.

RELATED PATTERNS

Interface   One form of coupling between classes is the coupling between a subclass and its superclass. It is often possible to avoid subclassing by using the Interface pattern described in Volume 1.

Mediator   It is not necessary or even always desirable for all of the classes in a design to have low coupling and high cohesion. Sometimes the overall complexity of a class can be reduced by concentrating complexity in one class. The Mediator pattern described in Volume 1 provides an example of this.

Composed Method   It is possible for methods to lack cohesion and be difficult to work with. Some common causes are excessive length or too many execution paths within a method. The Composed Method pattern provides guidance for breaking up such methods into smaller, simpler, and more cohesive methods.

Expert [Larman98]

Expert is the most frequently used pattern for assigning responsibilities.

SYNOPSIS

Assign a responsibility to the class that has the information required to carry out the responsibility.

CONTEXT

Suppose you are designing software for an employee timekeeping system. Analysis of the problem has produced a conceptual model that includes the three entities shown in Figure 4.5. The entities are responsible for determining the number of hours that an employee has worked in a pay period. During a pay period, an employee may work some shifts. The timekeeping events associated with a shift determine the number of hours that the employee worked during that shift. Your initial design includes a class to represent each of these entities, as shown in the class diagram in Figure 4.6.

The `PayPeriod` class has a `getMinutesWorked` method that corresponds to the `minutesWorked` attribute of the `PayPeriod` entity in the conceptual model. The `getMinutesWorked` method is responsible for finding out how many minutes an employee worked during each shift and adding up the total number of minutes for all the shifts in the pay period.

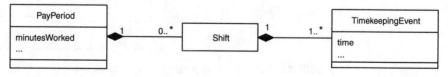

FIGURE 4.5 Timekeeping conceptual model.

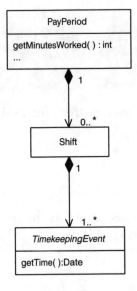

FIGURE 4.6 Basic pay period classes.

There is more than one way to assign the responsibilities for computing the result of the getMinutesWorked method. The interaction diagram in Figure 4.7 shows a rather literal approach. This diagram shows the PayPeriod class's getMinutesWorked method obtaining TimekeepingEvent objects from Shift objects and interpreting them so that it can determine how many minutes the employee worked in the pay period. This approach makes both the PayPeriod class and the Shift class dependent on the TimekeepingEvent class.

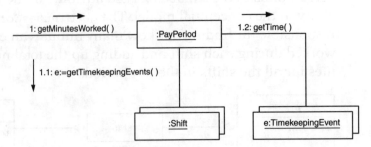

FIGURE 4.7 Literal assignment of responsibility.

The conceptual model does not contain any direct connections between pay periods and timekeeping events. This suggests that it is possible to assign the responsibilities for computing the result of the getMinutesWorked method without the PayPeriod class having a dependency on the TimekeepingEvent class.

Because timekeeping events define a shift, it seems clear that the Shift class will have dependencies on the TimekeepingEvent class no matter where the responsibilities for computing the result of the getMinutesWorked method are assigned. You realize that you can avoid making additional classes dependent on the TimekeepingEvent class by including the portion of the computation of minutes worked that involved timekeeping events in the Shift class. Figure 4.8 shows a collaboration diagram with this approach.

Using this approach, you assign responsibility to classes based on the information that they already have. Shift objects compute the number of minutes worked in the shift based on the TimekeepingEvent objects that they aggregate. PayPeriod objects simply request how many minutes were worked from each of the Shift objects that they aggregate and add up the shift totals.

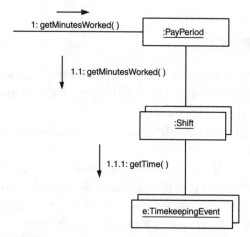

FIGURE 4.8 Responsibilities based on prior dependencies.

FORCES

- You want to assign a responsibility to a class.
- Unless there are indications to the contrary, you want to assign the responsibility to a class that is already present in your design, since adding classes without a reason adds complexity without any offsetting benefit.
- A class already has access to the information required to carry out a computation.
- You want to avoid or minimize additional dependencies between objects as you assign responsibilities to them.

SOLUTION

Assign a responsibility to the class or classes that have the information required to carry out the responsibility.

Often the expert classes correspond to the real-world entities that carry out those responsibilities, but not always. In the example included under the "Context" heading, we assigned the `Shift` class the responsibility of performing a computation. In the real world, shifts contain time but are not instruments of computation.

CONSEQUENCES

- Assigning responsibilities to classes that already have the information required to fulfill them maintains their encapsulation of that information.
- Avoiding new dependencies between classes promotes low coupling.
- Adding a method to a class because it already has data to support that method promotes highly cohesive classes.
- Assigning an excessive number of responsibilities to a class using the Expert pattern can cause the class to become excessively complex. It can even become highly coupled and uncohesive.

RELATED PATTERNS

Low Coupling/High Cohesion   The Expert pattern promotes low coupling by putting methods in the classes that have the information required by the methods. Classes whose methods require only the class's information have less need to rely on other classes. A set of methods that all operate on the same information tends to be cohesive.

Creator [Larman98]

SYNOPSIS

Determine which class should create instances of a class based on the relationship between the potential creator classes and the class to be instantiated.

CONTEXT

Suppose you are writing an employee timekeeping system. The purpose of the timekeeping system is to determine how many hours an employee works during a pay period. During a pay period an employee works for periods of time called *shifts*. The timekeeping system learns about the shifts worked by an employee as it receives timekeeping events. Figure 4.9 is a class diagram that shows the classes you will use to represent these entities.

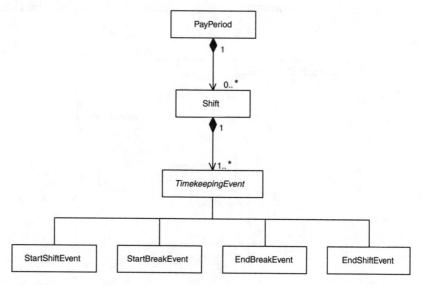

FIGURE 4.9 Timekeeping event classes.

This diagram shows that instances of the `PayPeriod` class compose instances of the `Shift` class. Instances of the `Shift` class compose instances of the abstract class `TimekeepingEvent`. The `TimekeepingEvent` class has a few concrete subclasses. Instances of the `TimekeepingEvent` subclasses represent the time that an employee started a shift, started a break, ended a break, or ended a shift.

You will need to decide which classes are responsible for creating instances of the `Shift` and `TimekeepingEvent` classes. The Creator pattern states that a class that composes or aggregates instances of another class is a good class to assign responsibility for creating instances of the composed or aggregated classes. Based on this, you decide to make the `PayPeriod` class responsible for creating instances of the `Shift` class. You also decide to make the `Shift` class responsible for creating instances of the `TimekeepingEvent` class. Based on those decisions, you design the collaborations shown in Figure 4.10.

FORCES

- When selecting a class that is responsible for creating instances of another class, it simplifies the design to choose

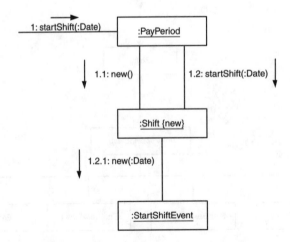

FIGURE 4.10 Timekeeping event creation.

a class whose instance requires a reference to the created object. If the class creates the object, it does not need to obtain a reference to it.

■ Suppose that one object uses a reference to another object. There is a greater likelihood that a class will be simplified (have lower coupling and higher cohesion) by creating the object it references when more of the object's lifetime is used for the reference. The nature of the relationship between the classes is a good basis for predicting how much of their lifetime a class's instances will need to use for a reference to an object.

SOLUTION

Class B should be responsible for creating instances of Class A if any of the following are true:

■ Class B and Class A are the same class and their instances compose, aggregate, contain, or directly use other instances of the same class.

■ Instances of Class B compose or aggregate instances of Class A.

■ Instances of Class B contain instances of Class A.

■ Instances of Class B record instances of Class A.

■ Instances of Class B directly use instances of Class A.

■ Instances of Class B have the data that is passed to constructors of Class A. Thus, the Expert pattern suggests making Class B responsible for creating instances of Class A.

When more than one of these relationships apply, choosing the one closer to the top of the list will usually produce the better result.

CONSEQUENCES

The creator pattern promotes low coupling by making instances of a class responsible for creating objects they need to reference.

By creating the object themselves, they avoid being dependent on another class to create the object for them.

RELATED PATTERNS

Composite   The Composite pattern described in Volume 1 describes a strong form of aggregation relationship.

Polymorphism [Larman98]

SYNOPSIS

When alternate behaviors are selected based on the type of an object, use a polymorphic method call to select the behavior, rather than using `if` statements to test the type.

CONTEXT

Suppose you are designing software for an employee timekeeping system that keeps track of the number of hours an employee works in a pay period. It does this by organizing the pay period into intervals of time that the employee works, called *shifts*.

The classes that you design include classes to represent shifts and pay periods. The pay period is responsible for breaking down the time worked into regular minutes and overtime minutes. The reason for this is that overtime minutes are paid at a higher rate than regular minutes. The class diagram in Figure 4.11 shows these classes.

The logic for breaking down an employee's time worked into regular minutes and overtime minutes will vary with the laws and

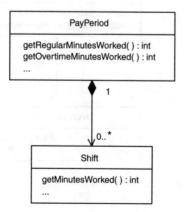

FIGURE 4.11 Pay period time reporting.

regulations of the locale where the employee works. You could use a chain of `if` statements to select the appropriate logic for breaking down time worked into regular and overtime minutes. The problem with a chain of `if` statements is that the longer the chain, the more opportunities there are to introduce bugs. Also, they make exhaustive unit testing more difficult (see the Unit Testing pattern) by adding more execution paths to test.

You decide, instead, to use a polymorphic method call because it will be easier to design and maintain. The class diagram in Figure 4.12 shows the additional classes for breaking down the time worked.

This class diagram shows that there is an instance of the `TimeTotaler` class associated with each `PayPeriod` object. Since `TimeTotaler` is an abstract class, the `TimeTotaler` object is actually an instance of a concrete subclass of `TimeTotaler`. When a `PayPeriod` object calls one of the `TimeTotaler` object's methods, the actual method that is called depends on the actual concrete subclass of `TimeTotaler` of which the object is an instance. The

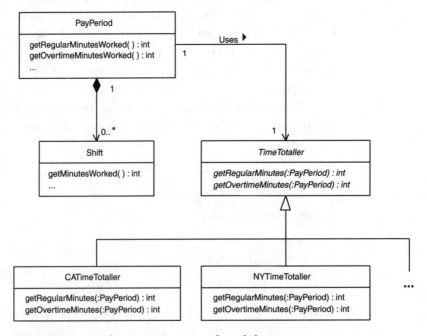

FIGURE 4.12 Regular/overtime time breakdown.

type of method call that makes the actual method called dependent on the actual class of an object is called a *polymorphic* method call.

FORCES

- It is always possible to select a behavior by using an explicit chain of `if` statements.
- When writing a chain of `if` statements, programmers have the opportunity to introduce bugs into a program. Later on, during maintenance, programmers have more opportunities to introduce bugs. A particularly common maintenance bug of this sort is adding a new behavior to some `if` statement chains, but neglecting to add it to others.
- The selection of a behavior by a polymorphic method call does not require a programmer to code any explicit logic. This allows fewer opportunities to introduce bugs.
- A chain of `if` statements makes it harder to exhaustively unit test a class by increasing the number of execution paths to be tested. The number of execution paths is multiplied by the length of the `if` statement chain.
- A polymorphic method call can be faster than a chain of `if` statements. Simply having a reference to an appropriate object provides access to the appropriate method implementation, without requiring any additional computation. The entire cost for a polymorphic method call is just the method call.
- You want to be able to include the mechanism for selecting a behavior in an object-oriented design. Chains of `if` statements have no natural representation in an object-oriented design.
- You can select an appropriate behavior from a set of alternatives by the class of an object.
- If a problem is stated in terms of selecting behavior based on a closed set of data values, you can enjoy the benefits of polymorphic method calls by organizing the solution to use a different class for each data value.

SOLUTION

If a problem is formulated in a way that implies the selection of behavior based on a data value from a closed set of data values, organize the solution to represent each data value with a different class. This allows the solution to select the behavior based on the class of an object.

If you can use the class of an object to select a behavior, then embed the desired behavior in the class and use polymorphic method calls to invoke the behavior.

CONSEQUENCES

- It is easier and more reliable to implement the selection of behavior using polymorphism than using explicit selection logic.
- Using polymorphism, it is easier to add additional behaviors later on because you don't have to hunt down the appropriate chains of `if` statements to which to add the behavior.
- Using the polymorphism pattern adds more classes to a design. This can make the design more difficult to understand in its entirety.
- Using a chain of `if` statements allows a programmer who is reading the code to see the possible choices. The use of polymorphic method calls makes that information more difficult to obtain.

RELATED PATTERNS

Dynamic Linkage   You can implement plug-ins or pluggable software components using a combination of polymorphism and the Dynamic Linkage pattern described in Volume 1.

Minimize Execution Paths   The Polymorphism pattern is a technique for implementing the Minimize Execution Paths pattern.

Pure Fabrication [Larman98]

SYNOPSIS

You must assign a responsibility to a class, but assigning it to a class that represents a conceptual model entity would ruin its low coupling or high cohesion. You resolve this problem by fabricating a class that does not represent an entity in your conceptual model.

CONTEXT

Suppose you have the task of designing an integrated system for managing an independent field service organization. This organization sends technicians who install and repair equipment on service calls to organizations that use the equipment. Some service calls are paid for by the organization that uses the equipment. The equipment vendors pay for some service calls as well. Others are paid for jointly by the equipment vendors and the user organization. Figure 4.13 shows part of the conceptual model for this service organization.

In this model, a service manager is given field service projects for a user organization. The project consists of tasks to be performed. The service manager schedules service technicians to perform the tasks, and periodically reviews the status of each project. The service manager sends invoices for the completed tasks to the paying organizations that are responsible for payment.

Creating classes that directly correspond to entities in a conceptual model provides you with a good first pass at a design. The class diagram in Figure 4.14 shows classes that correspond to the entities in the conceptual model with some of the responsibilities described previously. Looking at this class diagram, you notice that the `ServiceManager` class is rather highly coupled to the other classes in the diagram. Its methods do not serve a single cohesive purpose.

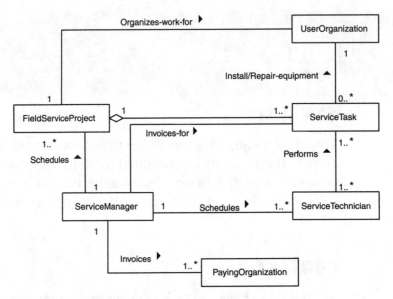

FIGURE 4.13 Field service conceptual model.

The responsibility for scheduling tasks is central to the function of the service manager. There is no class to reasonably give the responsibility for generating invoices, so you fabricate an additional class for this responsibility. The class diagram in Figure 4.15 shows this responsibility assigned to a fabricated class.

In this class diagram, you see the fabricated class `Invoice-Generator` added to the design and given the responsibility of invoicing the organizations that are responsible for payment for completed tasks. The result is that both the `ServiceManager` class and the `InvoiceGenerator` class are highly cohesive and have a lower level of coupling to other classes.

FORCES

- A responsibility must be added to an object-oriented design.

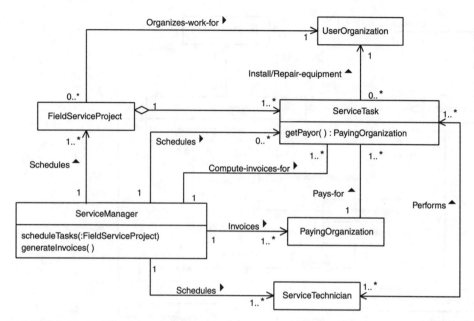

FIGURE 4.14 Field service classes.

- It is not possible to add the responsibility to any of the classes that represent conceptual model entities without damaging their low coupling or high cohesion.

SOLUTION

When making an initial assignment of responsibilities to classes, the simplest strategy is to assign the responsibilities to classes that correspond to entities created by the conceptual model during analysis. Sometimes, there is no such class to which you can add a responsibility and still maintain the class's low coupling and high cohesion. When this happens, create a class that is a pure fabrication, unrelated to any entity in the conceptual model.

CONSEQUENCES

- Using the Pure Fabrication pattern preserves the low coupling and high cohesion of the classes in an object-oriented design.

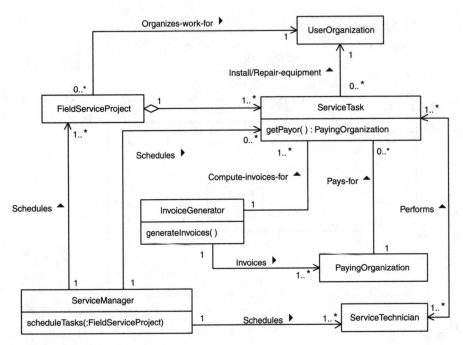

FIGURE 4.15 Fabricated field service classes.

- The reusability of the classes in a design can be improved because the Pure Fabrication pattern promotes the existence of classes that have fine-grained responsibility.

RELATED PATTERNS

Low Coupling/High Cohesion   The point of the Pure Fabrication pattern is to maintain the low coupling and high cohesion of the classes in an object-oriented design.

Law of Demeter [Larman98]

This pattern is also known as *Don't Talk to Strangers*.

SYNOPSIS

If two classes have no reason to be directly aware of each other or to be otherwise coupled, then the two classes should not directly interact. Instead of having a class call the methods of another class with which it has no reason to be coupled, you should have it call that method indirectly through another class. Insisting on such indirection keeps a design's overall level of coupling down.

CONTEXT

Suppose you are designing an employee timekeeping system. Your design, so far, includes the classes and associations shown in the class diagram in Figure 4.16. The purpose of the classes in this figure is to determine how many regular and overtime hours an employee worked in a given pay period. Here are descriptions of the classes shown in Figure 4.16:

Employee   Instances of the `Employee` class represent an employee.

PayrollRules   The rules for paying an employee vary with the laws that apply to the location where the employee works. They may also vary if the employee belongs to a union. Instances of the `PayrollRules` class encapsulate the pay rules that apply to an employee.

PayPeriod   Instances of the `PayPeriod` class represent a range of days for which an employee is paid in the same paycheck.

Shift   Instances of the `Shift` class represent ranges of time that the employee worked.

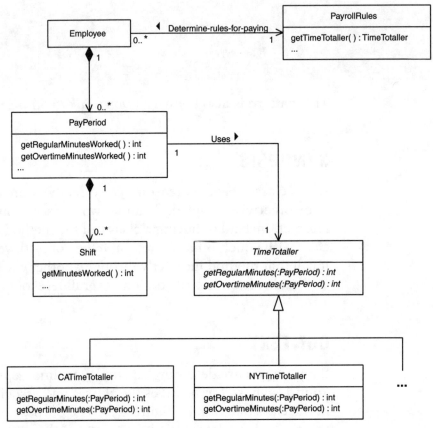

FIGURE 4.16 Time-totalling classes.

TimeTotaller   The `TimeTotaller` class is an abstract class that
   the `PayPeriod` class uses to break the total hours worked during a pay period into regular and overtime minutes.

CATimeTotaller and NYTimeTotaller   These are concrete subclasses of `TimeTotaller` that encapsulate the rules for breaking
   total minutes worked into regular and overtime minutes worked.
   Each of these classes encapsulates rules for a different locale.

   To make these classes carry out their responsibility for computing the number of regular and overtime minutes an employee
worked during a pay period, there are some interactions that
must occur for which the design does not account:

- The pay period must become associated with an instance of the subclass of `TimeTotaller` appropriate for the employee when the `PayPeriod` object is created.
- The `TimeTotaller` object must be able to examine each shift in the pay period to learn the number of minutes worked in each shift.

The Law of Demeter pattern states that classes that have no reason to be aware of each other should not have any direct interactions. Based on this, the class diagram in Figure 4.17 shows how these interactions should *not* be designed.

The `PayPeriod` class has no reason to know anything about the `PayrollRules` class. The `TimeTotaller` class does have a legitimate reason to be aware of the `Shift` class. However, for a `TimeTotaller` object to directly access the collection of shifts that it needs implies violation of the `Shift` class's encapsulation of how it aggregates collections of shifts. These direct interactions result in a higher level of coupling for the classes that are involved.

These interactions must be indirect in order to occur without creating problems in the design. The collaboration diagram in Figure 4.18 shows the interactions occurring in a way that respects the rest of the design.

The interactions in this diagram are less direct, but they respect the encapsulation of the classes involved and maintain a low level of coupling. The class diagram in Figure 4.19 shows the previous design with methods added to support the interactions of the diagram in Figure 4.18.

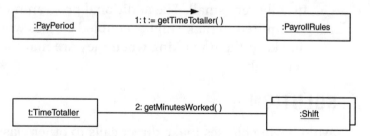

FIGURE 4.17 Bad time-totalling collaboration.

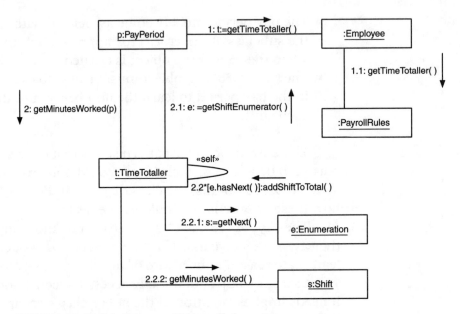

FIGURE 4.18 Good time-totalling collaboration.

FORCES

- Designing a class to directly access all the other classes whose services it needs is the most efficient organization of classes in terms of time spent accessing those services.
- Designing a class to directly access all the other classes whose services it requires can make the class highly coupled to other classes. It also makes the classes more likely to require a change if the structure of the relationships changes. It also makes the design less robust.
- The amount of time lost in making indirect method calls is usually very small. The additional programmer time that is required to make highly coupled classes work correctly and keep them working when they are maintained can be very high.

SOLUTION

Avoid having classes make direct calls to other classes with which they have an indirect relationship. Objects that follow this guide-

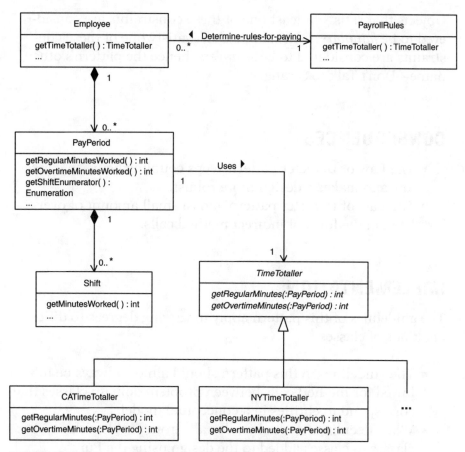

FIGURE 4.19 Enhanced time-totalling classes.

line should make method calls only to objects with which they have one of the following relationships:

- The same object (`this`)
- An object that is passed as a parameter to a method
- An object to which one of its instance variables directly refers
- An object in a collection to which one of its instance variables directly refers
- An object created by the object

Objects that satisfy at least one of these constraints are considered to be *familiars*. Objects that don't satisfy one of these constraints are considered to be *strangers*, hence the pattern's other name—Don't Talk to Strangers.

CONSEQUENCES

- The Law of Demeter pattern keeps coupling between classes low and makes a design more robust.
- The Law of Demeter pattern adds a small amount of overhead in the form of indirect method calls.

IMPLEMENTATION

The guidelines of this pattern apply in varying degrees to different kinds of classes.

- The guidelines in this pattern should almost always be followed for method calls between problem domain classes that correspond to entities in a conceptual model.
- When deciding how to handle calls from problem domain classes to classes added to the design using the Pure Fabrication pattern, there may be other considerations that justify direct calls between the otherwise unrelated classes. The Mediator pattern described in Volume 1 provides an example of this.
- Calls to utility classes that are not specific to the problem domain or the application are generally not subject to the guidelines of this pattern. The same applies to calls made between different architectural layers of a design.

RELATED PATTERNS

Low Coupling/High Cohesion The fundamental motivation for the Law of Demeter pattern is to maintain low coupling.

Pure Fabrication   There are sometimes good reasons why calls made to classes added to a design using the Pure Fabrication pattern should violate the guidelines of the Law of Demeter pattern.

Mediator   The Mediator pattern (described in Volume 1) provides an example of a class created through pure fabrication that receives direct method calls from classes unrelated to it with a benefit that outweighs the disadvantages of the direct calls.

Controller [Larman98]

SYNOPSIS

If a program receives events from external sources other than its graphical user interface, add an event class to decouple the event source(s) from the objects that actually handle the events.

CONTEXT

Suppose you are designing a security system. The security system is attached to numerous devices that sense the opening of doors and windows, motion within a building, and other events.

You don't want the external devices or the objects responsible for receiving the raw input from the devices to send any events directly to the objects within the security system that will handle the events. You want to avoid the direct coupling between them that would be required for direct delivery of such events.

To arrange for indirect coupling between external event sources and internal event handler classes, you include a controller class in the design. An instance of the controller class receives the events and dispatches them to the appropriate object to handle the event.

FORCES

- In order for an external event to be sent directly to the object within a program that handles that event, at least one of the objects must have a reference to the other. This can imply a very inflexible design if the event handler is dependent on the type of the event source or the event source is dependent on the type of the event handler.

- In the simplest case, the relationship between the external event source and the internal event handler consists purely of passing events. This situation is simple enough that interfaces can be used to provide the necessary type independence between the event source and the event handler. This is described in more detail in the discussion of the Interface pattern in Volume 1.
- Interfaces are not sufficient to provide behavioral independence between event sources and event handlers when the relationship between them is more complicated. For example, if some dispatching logic is required to decide which handler will be used for an event, you don't want to assign that responsibility to the external event sources. You want to keep them independent of any particular event-handling classes.

  If a response is required when an external event source enters an exceptional state, you don't want to assign that responsibility to the internal event-handling classes. At best, it would make them less cohesive. It could also add some level of dependency between them.
- You can avoid dependencies between external event sources and internal event handlers by interposing an object between them to act as an intermediary for event delivery. The object should be able to manage any other complicating facets of the relationship.

SOLUTION

Make an object responsible for receiving external events and forwarding them to the appropriate internal event-handling object. Such an object that coordinates external events is called a *controller* object. This arrangement is shown in Figure 4.20.

CONSEQUENCES

- Using a controller object keeps external event sources and internal event handlers independent of each other's type and behavior.

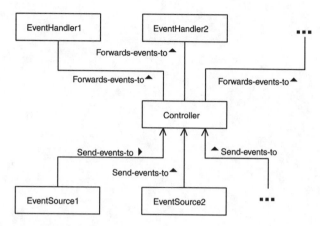

FIGURE 4.20 Controller class.

■ As a design evolves, it is common for the design of controller objects to become highly coupled and uncohesive. This happens as they are assigned responsibilities for forwarding different kinds of events from different kinds of external event sources to different kinds of internal event handlers.

This is not necessarily evidence of a design problem. Sometimes a highly coupled and uncohesive controller object results in less overall complexity than if the controller object were split into multiple objects. If the controller object encapsulates state information used to manage relationships between multiple event sources and handlers, then you are usually better off not splitting the controller up into multiple objects that are less highly coupled.

RELATED PATTERNS

Pure Fabrication   The Controller pattern is a specialized form of the Pure Fabrication pattern.

Mediator   The Mediator pattern is used to coordinate events from a GUI. Like controller objects, a highly coupled and uncohesive mediator object may involve less overall complexity than an arrangement that distributes the same responsibilities over more objects.

C H A P T E R

5

GUI Design Patterns

The patterns in this chapter provide direction for the design of graphical user interfaces (GUIs). The GUI patterns discussed here differ from the patterns found in the other chapters in this book in that they are based, to a larger extent, on common design practices rather than on pragmatic considerations.

The patterns in this chapter solve GUI-related design problems. When you design a GUI with these patterns you are likely to use some of them together, and it's not unusual to use some of the patterns more than once. Some of the GUI requirements that these patterns help to meet follow.

Use elements that are familiar to the user in the GUI.
GUIs that use widgets and conventions that are already familiar to new users are easier to grasp because the users will possess knowledge and expectations that are consistent with their use. For example, users will usually know what to do if they see a pop-up menu like the one in Figure 5.1. A pie menu, like the one shown in Figure 5.2, can reduce the needed mouse motion if it pops up with its center right under the mouse pointer. However, pie menus are very unusual, so users may not know what to do the first time they see one.

Users are also less likely to make mistakes if their existing habits and expectations work with a new GUI.

Design GUI components that are consistent with users' expectations and knowledge base. Users are surprised when the result of an interaction with a GUI is not what they expect. A GUI that reduces unexpected reactions from the user is easier to learn to use. It also causes less frustration and fewer errors. When different parts of a GUI behave inconsistently, the level of perceived surprise is higher and users take longer to learn

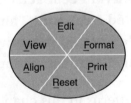

FIGURE 5.1 Pop-up menu.   **FIGURE 5.2** Pie menu.

to use the new interface. Conversely, when a GUI behaves in a way that seems consistent, it reinforces users' confidence in those portions of the user interface that seem familiar. For example, suppose a user begins to use a drawing program and discovers that double-clicking on a shape brings up a dialog for editing the shape's properties. As the user continues to use that feature with different shapes and gets consistent results, the user gains confidence in the feature. If the user then clicks on a previously unused shape and the program zooms in instead of popping up a dialog, the user will be surprised and unsure of what to do. The user will also be less confident about double-clicking on shapes in general.

A well-designed GUI forgives user mistakes.   When a GUI does not offer the user a way to recover from a mistake, the cost of that mistake can be very high. If the cost of mistakes is high, users become anxious, causing them to work more slowly or produce more errors. A user interface that gives users the opportunity to recover from mistakes builds user confidence, and this usually results in improved productivity and fewer mistakes.

For example, consider a drawing program that allows multiple shapes to be cut or pasted simultaneously. This is a powerful feature that can improve a user's productivity. However, it is very important that the user be able to undo those operations. Having to manually undo the effect of a multishape cut or paste operation is time consuming. It would discourage users from using these features. It might also discourage users from experimenting with other features.

The GUI must provide warnings to the users for those operations that cannot be undone.   If a GUI allows users to recover from most mistakes, users will expect it to allow them to recover from all mistakes. If a GUI that allows users to recover from most mistakes does not provide a warning before performing an operation that cannot be undone, the users may be unpleasantly surprised.

Consider a word processor that has commands to automatically format an entire document. The word processor has an undo command that is able to undo most other commands. But because there is no upper bound on the number of changes the automatic formatting command can make to a document, the word processor's undo mechanism will not undo the results of the automatic formatting command.

The word processor pops up a dialog to warn users that the command cannot be undone before it executes the command. This warning allows the user to avoid a very undesirable situation that could occur if the user meant to issue a different command than the one that reformats an entire document. Without the warning, clicking on the wrong menu item could result in reformatting an entire document, with the user having no idea how the document changed so drastically and facing the task of manually reformatting the entire document.

A GUI must walk users through unfamiliar tasks step by step. The user should always be able to determine the next step in performing common tasks. In cases where the instructions slow down an experienced user, there should also be a mechanism that places the coaching out of the user's way.

Provide short cuts to routine tasks for experienced users. If speed of use is an issue, experienced users who regularly use a GUI should be able to perform routine tasks quickly.

Most of the patterns presented in this chapter work together to address these requirements. They provide basic guidelines for designing a user-centered GUI. Figure 5.3 is a map that shows how the GUI design patterns in this chapter fit together.

Here is a summary of the 12 GUI patterns described in this chapter:

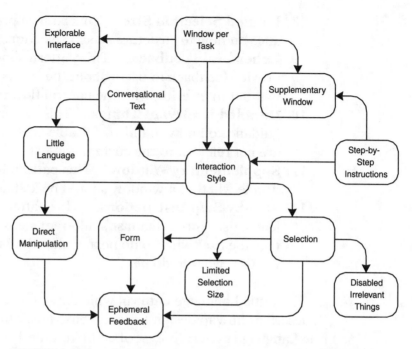

FIGURE 5.3 Map of GUI design patterns discussed in Chapter 5.

1. **Window per Task.**   This pattern tells you to organize a user interface into windows dedicated to different tasks.
2. **Interaction Style.**   This pattern helps you select the primary way in which users interact with a window.
3. **Explorable Interface.**   This pattern provides guidance on minimizing the costs of users' mistakes.
4. **Conversational Text.**   This pattern describes how users can interact with a window by entering text-based commands. The *Little Language* pattern described in Volume 1 shows how to design and implement textual command input as a little language.
5. **Selection.**   This pattern describes a style of user interaction where the user chooses selections from a list.
6. **Form.**   This pattern describes how to collect information from a user in a structured way.
7. **Direct Manipulation.**   This pattern provides guidance on how to structure user interactions with domain-specific metaphors.

8. **Limited Selection Size.**   This pattern provides guidance on how to structure sets of selections.

9. **Ephemeral Feedback.**   This pattern shows how to provide feedback to users about the status of their work, without interfering with the natural flow of their work.

10. **Disabled Irrelevant Things.**   This pattern provides guidance on how to hide or disable GUI elements that are not relevant to the current context.

11. **Supplementary Window.**   This pattern helps you decide whether a window should be a dialog.

12. **Step-by-Step Instructions.**   This pattern shows how to lead a user through a task's different steps when the GUI tells the user what to do next, rather than the user telling the GUI what to do next.

The Little Language pattern, which is also shown in Figure 5.3, describes how to design textually based user interfaces. The Little Language pattern is described in Volume 1.

Window Per Task [Beck-Cunningham87]

SYNOPSIS

A GUI should have a separate window for each cohesive task a user must perform. All information required to perform the task should be available from the window. The application provides a way to navigate between windows, allowing the user to coordinate tasks.

CONTEXT

Suppose you are designing a GUI for an integrated development environment. It must support programmers in a number of tasks, such as editing code, painting screens, and debugging. It will also need to support these tasks concurrently, so that programmers can seamlessly move from editing code to debugging and back again. To support these types of multiple tasks concurrently, the GUI must display the tasks at the same time and allow programmers to navigate from one task to another.

You decide to organize the tasks the GUI will allow the user to perform by associating each task with a window. You base the organization of the windows on the principles of high cohesion and low coupling. Putting multiple tasks in a window would couple the tasks, making the contents of the window uncohesive and more difficult to understand.

A better solution is to present only one task in each window, allowing the purpose of each window to be evident. When the purpose of each window is clear, it is easier to navigate between windows.

FORCES

- If a window contains elements that perform different or unrelated tasks, the window is not cohesive and is difficult for users to understand. It can also make it difficult for users to find the appropriate location within the GUI to perform a task, and can cause users to be confused as to which element of a window is related to a given task.

For example, consider a window that is used for both spell checking and printing documents. Suppose that it has a field labeled "number of copies." The intention of the field is to specify the number of copies to be printed. The spell checker can detect duplicate words, such as "the the." Because the same window is used for spell checking and printing, when the spell checker reports duplicate words, that report appears in the same window as a field that may say "Number of copies: 1." A user might misinterpret the purpose of this printing-related field as referring to duplicate word detection.

- If a window is dedicated to a single task, then the presentation of that task is not coupled to other tasks. The presentation of a task in a dedicated window is automatically more cohesive than a presentation of multiple tasks in the same window.
- When there is a one-to-one relationship between tasks and windows, it is easier to find the window that is associated with a specific task.

SOLUTION

Provide each major task with its own window. Each window should have navigational tools, such as menu items and push buttons, to allow users to navigate to other windows. The windows should work together without requiring users to quit tasks to reach another window.

CONSEQUENCES

If each window is dedicated to a specific task, the presentation of the task is simplified and it is easier to find the window that presents a specific task.

RELATED PATTERNS

Low Coupling/High Cohesion   The Task per Window pattern is based on the principles of low coupling and high cohesion.

Interaction Style [Coram-Lee98]

SYNOPSIS

Match the GUI's interaction style to the abilities of its users and the application's requirements. The most common styles of interaction are selection, form, direct manipulation, and conversational text.

CONTEXT

Suppose you are designing a GUI that allows people to query a relational database which contains ingredient and nutritional information for food items in a supermarket. A supermarket has requested this application to help its customers select products.

The most flexible style of GUI for querying a relational database is based on *conversational text*. It allows people to type in queries as Structured Query Language (SQL) and then shows the results of the query. Though well suited to the requirements of the application, a GUI based on conversational text is not appropriate for the users of this application. This style of GUI requires a good knowledge of SQL and an understanding of the database's structure. Most supermarket customers are unlikely to have or want to acquire either skill, so you rule out conversational text for this particular GUI design.

A GUI based on *selections* allows users to make a series of decisions by selecting from lists of choices. This style of interaction is not well suited to the requirements of the application, because the application is supposed to allow supermarket customers to ask about foods that contain arbitrary combinations of ingredients and nutrients. Selections cannot contain arbitrary combinations of things and still be reasonable in size.

A GUI based on *forms* allows users to enter information in a structured way that helps them supply the necessary information. This style of interaction suits your purpose for the GUI, and you decide to use a form as the primary style of interaction. You envision a GUI that has a form that corresponds to each type of query that you think will be useful in the application. You also envision using selection interactions for portions of the GUI to allow users to select the type of query they are interested in and to select specific nutrients and ingredients to enter into the forms. To tie it all together, you use the Step-by-Step Instructions pattern, which is described later in this chapter.

FORCES

There are four common styles of interaction with GUIs:

1. *Selection* interactions allow a user to select a data value or the next action to perform from a list.
2. *Form* interactions allow a user to provide information or specify what to do by filling in the fields of a form.
3. A *direct manipulation* style of interaction provides a visual representation of the task performed and various commands to direct the task. Word processors usually follow this form of interaction. Direct manipulation is usually combined with selection so that less commonly used commands are available through menus or tool bars.
4. *Conversational text* interactions allow a user to enter complex commands as text.

Other styles of interaction with GUIs are possible but uncommon. By sticking to the four styles of interaction described here, you greatly increase the likelihood that the basic operating concepts of your GUI will already be familiar to your users.

Some types of applications commonly use other styles of interaction. For example, many computer games have a GUI that requires the user to respond to events in a simulated environment, such as a racetrack or a boxing ring. Such styles of interaction are good design choices for applications where users are already familiar with the style of interaction.

Using a style of interaction that is unfamiliar to new users may dramatically increase their initial level of anxiety about learning to use a new GUI, as well as the amount of time it takes them to learn to use it.

Selecting an interaction style for a GUI that is not appropriate for the needs of an application will result in an application that is difficult to learn and to use.

Note that the style of interaction is distinct from the way a GUI actually presents it. Although there are common ways of presenting each style of interaction, you will have choices to make in that area. For example, a simple selection interaction can be presented as pull-down menus, a set of buttons, or a set of hyperlinks.

SOLUTION

Choose the primary interaction style for a GUI:

- Choose selection interactions to guide users through well-defined tasks or choices.
- Choose form interactions when an application must collect specific types of information from users.
- Choose direct manipulation interactions to provide users with a visual representation of the task performed.
- Choose conversational text interaction for complex commands entered by highly trained knowledge workers.

If another style of interaction is common for the type of application that you are building, then consider that as an additional alternative to the four listed here.

As you develop portions of the GUI to perform different tasks or present different views of what is happening, you may discover portions of the GUI for which the primary style of interaction is inappropriate. Reapply this pattern to select an appropriate style of interaction for those portions of the GUI.

CONSEQUENCES

- Matching the style of interaction to the needs of the application simplifies the task of designing a GUI that works for its intended users.
- Matching the style of interaction to the needs of users results in a design that users find easier to learn because it has familiar elements.
- In applications that users use heavily, the ease of learning the application may be less important than the speed and accuracy that users can achieve during extended use. For such programs, nonstandard forms of interaction that promote speed and accuracy may be the most appropriate.

RELATED PATTERNS

Conversational Text   This pattern describes one of the interaction styles that the Interaction Style pattern promotes.

Form   This pattern describes one of the interaction styles that the Interaction Style pattern promotes.

Direct Manipulation   This pattern describes one of the interaction styles that the Interaction Style pattern promotes.

Selection   This pattern describes one of the interaction styles that the Interaction Style pattern promotes.

Step-by-Step Instructions   The Step-by-Step Instruction pattern may be used to specify a sequence of interaction modes.

Explorable Interface [Coram-Lee98]

SYNOPSIS

Design user interaction to forgive a user's mistakes by allowing the user to undo actions and go back to previous decision points.

CONTEXT

A good GUI must forgive users' mistakes. The cost of a mistake is low if a GUI allows the user to recover from the mistake. There are common methods to allow users to recover from mistakes, such as an undo facility or the ability to revert the state of the user's work to a previously saved state. It is often possible to design a GUI to provide mistake recovery throughout all or most of itself.

FORCES

- If a GUI does not provide any easy and effective mistake recovery mechanism, its users will be reluctant to explore features or procedures that they have not used before. This sort of reluctance impedes one of the most effective methods for users to improve their skills with a GUI—experimenting with features.
- If a GUI does not provide a method to recover from mistakes, the cost of mistakes is higher and so is the cost of paying someone to get work done using that GUI.
- Designing mistake recovery into a GUI decreases the average time it takes for users to perform tasks, because the delays that result from mistakes are much smaller than they would otherwise be. It also decreases the time needed to learn how to use a program because users are less anxious about mak-

ing mistakes and are more willing to explore the GUI without knowing what each command or action does.

■ Providing close to universal mistake recovery in a GUI leads users to expect that the GUI will allow them to recover from all mistakes. If this is not the case, the GUI should warn the user before proceeding with an operation from which it will not allow the user to recover.

SOLUTION

After performing a task, the GUI should allow the user to undo the effects of that task. Implementing the following measures accomplishes this for most conversational text, selection, form, and direct manipulation interactions:

■ After a command is given to a GUI that changes the state of a program, ensure that an undo command is available that will undo the effects of the last command. This is the most common mechanism for recovering from mistakes that result from a direct manipulation or conversational text interaction.

■ Some selection interactions choose a command and then perform it. In many cases it is appropriate for an undo operation to be available after the command has been performed. However, some selection interactions, such as hyperlink-based selection interactions, end by initiating another selection interaction. In such situations, it is customary for the selection interactions to include an option with a name like *Back* or *Go Back*. The option is intended to convey to users the idea of returning to the previous selection interaction. Within a program, Go Back operations are the same as undo operations.

■ Some tasks must be preceded by steps that specify the parameters of the task. It is common for GUIs to use dialogs for this purpose. A common mechanism for specifying parameters for a direct manipulation interaction is to select one or more objects in the GUI's display that are parameters for the task.

GUIs should provide a way to abort the specification of parameters and thereby avoid performing the originally requested task. If the parameters are gathered using a dialog, the dialog should have a Cancel button for aborting the dialog. In the case of a direct manipulation interaction, no explicit abort action is usually necessary. Users are usually able to abort the setup for a task and the task itself by simply doing something else.

- Both undo and abort actions apply to form interactions. When the purpose of a form interaction is to collect information, the GUI should include a Cancel button to abort the interaction. When the purpose of a form interaction is to edit information, the GUI should include a Reset button. The purpose of the Reset button is to restore the values displayed in the GUI to their original values.

    Note that there is no reason for GUIs that present form interactions to not have both Cancel and Reset buttons.

To minimize surprise to users, GUIs that provide mistake recovery for most interactions should warn the user before proceeding with any action from which they cannot provide recovery.

CONSEQUENCES

- Users spend minimal time recovering from mistakes.
- Users feel empowered to learn through trial and error.

IMPLEMENTATION

Sometimes users make a mistake, but do not immediately realize the mistake. Between the time that they make the mistake and the time they discover it, they may have used the GUI to perform multiple tasks. An undo facility that allows only the very last task to be undone is not adequate in these situations. To provide users with a good level of comfort, an undo mechanism must allow multiple commands to be undone.

Implementations of undo facilities usually place some limit on how many tasks can be undone, in order to limit the amount of memory required to remember how to undo tasks. Such a limit can be a rude surprise to a user who had previously been able to rely on the undo facility as a perfect safety net. Though imposing limits on the number of tasks that can be undone may be a practical necessity, the limit should be as high as possible.

For some types of programs, it may not be possible to provide an undo mechanism that is or appears to be reliable. For such programs, it is best to design the undo mechanism to be consistent in what it performs, so that the user's expectations for backing out of a situation are realistic before entering the situation. For example, most Web browsers have a Back button that does not undo or stop downloads.

A user might request an undo in error. For that reason, there should be a redo command that can negate undo operations.

It is possible to make the relationship between undo and redo sophisticated and complicated. For example, some programs allow users to undo some commands, enter a different command than they entered originally, and then redo the rest. Such sophisticated redo mechanisms can confuse users, so it is best to keep redo mechanisms simple unless you expect users to be trained on how to use them.

RELATED PATTERNS

Command   The Command pattern described in Volume 1 shows a way to undo the effects of a command or the performance of a task.

Conversational Text   The Explorable Interface pattern is often used with the Conversational Text pattern.

Form   The Explorable Interface pattern is often used with the Form pattern.

Supplementary Window   The Explorable Interface pattern is often used with the Supplementary Window pattern.

Direct Manipulation   The Explorable Interface pattern is often used with the Direct Manipulation pattern.

Selection The Selection pattern is often used with the Dialog pattern.

Snapshot The Snapshot pattern described in Volume 1 can be used to restore the state of a program to what it was at a previous time.

Conversational Text [Grand99]

SYNOPSIS

Design a GUI to accept commands in the form of textual input.

CONTEXT

Suppose you are designing a GUI front end to manage a network router. Because the router itself understands textual commands, the GUI will send textual commands to the router. Correctly entering the textual commands requires a high degree of familiarity, so the primary interaction style provided by the GUI will be a selection. The selection style of interaction guides the user through the process of formulating commands. It makes it easier for casual users to send commands to a router.

However, experienced users who feel comfortable with textually based commands find that in some cases it is faster and easier for them to type textual commands than it is to navigate through a hierarchy of menus. It is also convenient for them to store commonly used sequences of commands in a file and paste them into the GUI when they want to use them.

To support command entry, you set aside a separate area of the GUI for entering textual commands. You design this area of the GUI to support the customary text-editing commands for data entry fields, including pasting text.

In addition to allowing command entry, you design the command area to display the last command generated from a selection-based interaction. This shows those users who use menus to enter their commands what they could have typed instead of using the menu option.

FORCES

- Using a GUI-based mechanism to specify a command usually results in an obvious and easy-to-use interface if the command takes a fixed set of parameters. If the command is able to take arbitrary combinations of parameters, a GUI-based mechanism for specifying the command may be too complex for many users to use. Alternatively, it may attain a reasonable level of complexity by not providing enough expressiveness to specify all possible combinations of parameters.

- If a command structure is very complex, it may be faster and more expressive to enter a command as text than to specify the command through a sequence of forms and/or menu selections.

- For some applications, the GUI is required to execute a previously stored sequence of commands. One mechanism used for this is called a *macro*. The GUI typically creates macros by recording and saving commands as the user enters them. Later, the sequence of commands stored as a macro can be replayed.

  Macros have some shortcomings. In particular, mechanisms for editing a macro or for inspecting the sequence of commands that constitute it may be difficult for casual users to understand. Mechanisms that allow the user to edit a sequence of commands generally require the user to think of commands as abstract actions that are not tied to the specific data they were used with when recorded. That degree of abstraction is difficult for some users.

  A sequence of commands that is stored as text does not have this problem. You can inspect and edit it using any text-editing tool.

SOLUTION

Allow the user to enter complex commands into a GUI as text.

CONSEQUENCES

- Text-based commands are more difficult to learn than most other GUI interaction styles. When a user enters a text-based command, syntax errors are possible that are not possible with other styles of interaction. GUIs that provide autocompletions and suggestions for what to type next can help, but they do not eliminate the problem.

- A conversational text style of interaction provides less feedback than other styles of interaction. As a user enters a command there is no feedback about its validity. Other styles of interaction are able to provide immediate feedback as a command is formed. The feedback may take the form of grayed-out widgets to indicate that certain commands or options are not valid in the current context.

   Because textual commands are usually less connected with what a GUI displays than are other styles of interaction, there is often less direct feedback about the results of a textual command.

- If a mechanism for specifying commands textually does not already exist, you have to design the grammar for the commands themselves and create a mechanism to interpret the commands.

IMPLEMENTATION

Responses to textual commands are also textual in many cases. You may need to decide if it makes more sense to append responses to the same window in which commands are entered or to display the responses in a separate area. If there is no clear reason to prefer one arrangement over the other, as is often the case, you can resolve the decision by letting the user decide.

If a GUI allows both a conversational text mode of interaction and another way of specifying commands, the GUI may display the textual equivalent of each command that is entered through other means. This is a way of teaching users how to enter commands textually. Such a feature is helpful only for users who use a program often enough to learn and retain its nuances.

If a GUI is part of a program that has no special text-editing features, users will not expect the area for entering textual commands to have any special text-editing commands. However, if the GUI is part of a program that does have special text-editing features, such as a word processor, users are likely to expect the area for entering textual commands to have some of those features. To minimize surprise, the area for entering textual commands should allow as many of the program's text-manipulating features as make sense.

RELATED PATTERNS

Explorable Interface   The Explorable Interface pattern describes a technique for making a conversational text interaction more useable.

Interaction Style   The Interaction Style pattern is used to decide to use the Conversational Text pattern.

Little Language   The Little Language pattern described in Volume 1 shows how to design and implement textual command input as a little language.

Selection [Grand99]

SYNOPSIS

Allow users to interact with a GUI by selecting commands and data values from lists.

CONTEXT

Suppose you are designing a GUI for a kiosk in an airport that can be used to obtain information about hotels, restaurants, and points of interest around town. Because most user input will consist of choosing from lists of alternatives, the obvious choice for the GUI's primary interaction style is selection.

The GUI presents selection interactions in several different ways:

- You can select the types of establishments, such as hotels, restaurants, or local transportation, that interest the user. The GUI can reasonably present that information as an array of buttons.
- The GUI will allow the user to select a restaurant by the type of cuisine it serves. The GUI can present this set of choices as a scrollable list.
- The GUI will allow the user to select a hotel by the part of town it's in. A graphic way of presenting this set of choices is as an image map of the city. Clicking on an area of the map selects a list of hotels in and around the area.
- When presenting a description of a hotel, the GUI will offer the ability to present more information about the points of interest mentioned in the description, such as banquet facilities or the health club. The GUI can present these options as hyperlinks.

FORCES

- The user must specify a command or some data.
- The GUI knows, in advance, the set of commands or data values that the user may select.
- An application requires no data entry or has very simple data entry requirements that are satisfied by selecting values.
- Users often find it easier to select from a set of choices than to enter one into a blank field.

SOLUTION

Present a set of choices in a GUI and allow the user to select from them. Pointing and pressing buttons on a keyboard are the usual methods for users to indicate their selections.

There are two forms of selection style interaction:

1. *Single selection* allows a user to select no more than one choice from a set of choices. This is the more common of the two methods.
2. *Multiple selection* allows a user to select any number of choices from a list of choices.

There are two common presentation styles for selections:

1. A *flat presentation* displays all of the selections at once, equally.
2. A *hierarchical presentation* displays the selections as a hierarchy, where it may be necessary to select a higher-level item in the hierarchy before seeing a lower-level item.

CONSEQUENCES

- A GUI can use selections to guide users through tasks. By first presenting the user with a selection of tasks and then any additional selections that correspond to the decisions made in performing the task, the user is never left wondering, "What do I do next?" Other forms of interaction usually impose less structure on tasks. The higher level of a structure can be helpful to new or casual users of a GUI, but may slow down experienced users when performing routine tasks.

- It can take a long time to navigate through large numbers of choices.
- Selections can be used to simulate a keyboard, but this is very awkward to use.

IMPLEMENTATION

There are numerous ways that a GUI can present the choices in a simple selection interaction. The more common ones are described here.

- Pull-down or pop-up menus are useful for GUIs that use a selection style of interaction to supplement another style of interaction. Figures 5.4 and 5.5 show examples of a pull-down menu and a pop-up menu.

    Pull-down menus are used for selection interactions that modify the course of a user interaction in progress or initiate a new user interaction. Pop-up menus are typically used as a shortcut for an interaction that can be accomplished from a pull-down menu with additional steps.

FIGURE 5.4 Pull-down menu.   **FIGURE 5.5** Pop-up menu.

■ An array of buttons is a common way to present a selection interaction when selection is the GUI's primary interaction style and the purpose of the selection is to choose the next task or interaction. By its nature, this type of selection interaction is always of the single-selection variety. Figure 5.6 shows an example of a button array.

When an array of buttons is used to present a selection, it is normally the most prominent feature that the GUI presents.

The GUI can also display secondary features at the same time it presents a button array. You will often see a graphical element used to emphasize that the buttons are a cohesive group that form the main features of the GUI; for example, a box around the buttons.

■ An image map is another way to present a selection interaction. An image map is presented as an image. The appearance of an image map depends entirely on the image that it uses. The GUI logically, but not visually, divides the image up into visually distinct areas. When the user clicks on the image, the GUI interprets the click based on which area was clicked.

Image maps are used to select a task to be performed or to select data values. An example of an image map could be a picture that depicts different types of merchandise on a shelf. Clicking on a particular type of merchandise indicates that the user wants to know more about that merchandise or wants to select it for purchase.

FIGURE 5.6 Button array selection.

An example of an image map used to select data values could be a picture of an automobile that appears in a GUI used by insurance adjusters. The adjuster can click on different parts of the automobile to indicate areas of body damage.

■ List boxes are used to implement selection interactions that choose data values. List boxes present all the possible choices of a selection interaction using a single GUI component. List boxes are suitable for single-selection and multiple-selection interactions. An example of a list box appears in Figure 5.7.

The Limited Selection Size pattern found later in this chapter provides additional guidelines for when to use check boxes or radio buttons instead of a list box.

■ Check boxes and radio buttons are used to implement selection interactions that select data values or tasks. Both check boxes and radio buttons present possible choices of a selection interaction using a distinct GUI component.

Radio buttons are used to present a single-selection interaction. Check boxes are used to present a multiple-selection interaction. Figures 5.8 and 5.9 show examples of radio buttons and check boxes.

There is no significance to the arrangement of the radio buttons or check boxes. However, it is customary to arrange them in a row, column, or rectangle. To visually emphasize that the radio buttons or check boxes in a set are related, it is common for the GUI to draw a rectangle around them.

■ Hyperlinks are yet another way of presenting a selection interaction. The appearance of hyperlinks is entirely dependent on the browser that presents them. Words that are part of a hyperlink are usually displayed in a different color than the surrounding text and are underlined.

FIGURE 5.7 List box.

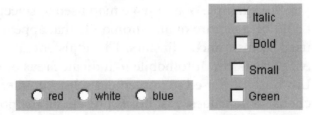

FIGURE 5.8 Radio buttons.   **FIGURE 5.9** Check boxes.

There are also a number of ways to present hierarchical selection interactions. Presentations of hierarchical selection interactions are more dynamic in nature, so we do not attempt to provide pictures of them. Descriptions of some of the more common presentations of hierarchical selections follow:

- Some selections are organized into a hierarchy because there would be an unreasonable number of items to choose from if they were all presented at one level. Selections that are organized into a hierarchy for organizational convenience are usually presented as cascading menus.

    The use of cascading menus can make it easier to find a command if the hierarchy is shallow and its organization is obvious. However, a hierarchy that is too deep or does not match the application in an obvious way can make it more difficult for users to find menu items than with a flat menu structure.

- If the hierarchy of the selections is part of the information in the selection, rather than an organizational convenience, then the selection is usually presented as a tree. A common example of this is an interaction for selecting a file in a hierarchical file system. This type of interaction usually presents the hierarchy of directories as a tree that expands to show lower-level directories when the user selects a directory.

- If the levels of a data hierarchy are few and fixed in meaning, a multipane browser is a common way to present the selection. For example, a tool for browsing Java methods may have a pane for selecting a package. Next to that pane would be a pane for selecting classes within the selected package. Next to that pane would be a pane for selecting methods within the selected class.

- If there is a lot of information to be presented that is related to each selection, hyperlinks embedded in the information can be the best way to present a hierarchical selection.

Many other ways of presenting selection interactions are possible. Some of them are specialized for selecting a particular kind of data or working with a particular type of pointing device. The presentation selected should be the presentation best adapted to the application. Unfortunately, a more comprehensive exploration of methods to present selections and to choose a presentation is beyond the scope of this chapter.

RELATED PATTERNS

Explorable Interface   The Explorable Interface pattern describes a technique for making a selection interaction more useable.

Limited Selection Size   The Limited Selection Size pattern provides additional guidance in determining the presentation of a selection interaction.

Form [Tidwell98]

SYNOPSIS

Allow a user to enter structured data into a GUI as discrete pieces of information.

CONTEXT

Suppose you are designing a GUI that allows people to fill out employment applications. The pieces of information obtained through the GUI must be discrete, meaning that an applicant's name, address, telephone number, and so on can be placed in separate fields of a database. The simplest way to capture discrete pieces of information from a GUI is to design it so that users provide the information in discrete pieces.

GUIs that capture discrete pieces of information are called *forms*. They are usually modeled on paper forms. Figure 5.10 shows a form that you can use for this application.

FORCES

- The GUI must allow the user to supply or edit specific and discrete pieces of information, such as address, city, state, and postal code. Unstructured data entry, such as with a word processor, will not do.
- To successfully supply information to the GUI, the user must know what information the GUI expects. The user should be able to tell which pieces of information the GUI requires and which pieces of information it considers optional. This is most important when the user may not be familiar with the GUI and certain information is unavailable.

  For example, the form in Figure 5.10 requests name, social security, and address information.

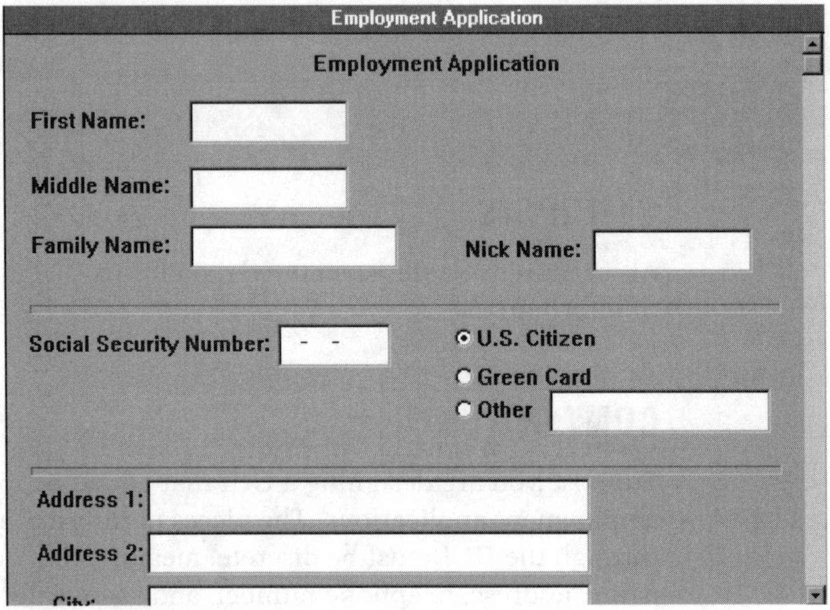

FIGURE 5.10 Employment application form.

- The GUI should provide any additional information that allows the user to enter acceptable data on the first try. Such information may appear as default data in a data entry field that provides the user with an example of the format in which data is expected. A field that contains today's date is an example of the expected data format. Explanatory text may appear directly in the form itself, if it is brief, or be available as help text that can be accessed by such means as a button press or a mouse click.
- Many users avoid reading directions. Though clear and explicit instructions may be included in a form, many users will not read the instructions or will skim over them without absorbing their full detail.
- There must be a way for the GUI to tell when the user is finished supplying or entering data. This is commonly accomplished with an OK or Submit button for the user to press when finished.
- If the information a user provides is not valid, the GUI should notify the user as soon as is practical. Early notification may

allow the user to more quickly fix the problem and move on. The more time that elapses between the input of the invalid data and the GUI's notification to the user of the problem, the more wasted effort the user may have expended. Also, as the user moves on to other pieces of data, it takes longer for the user to return to the source of the invalid piece of data.

■ If an inconsistent combination of values is provided on a form, it can be annoying and distracting for the GUI to notify the user before it is certain that the user is finished editing the values. Such premature notifications are usually false alarms that distract the user who has entered or edited some of the values and plans to finish the rest.

This sort of situation can happen when the user is editing the minimum and maximum values for a range of values. After entering the minimum value, but before entering the maximum value, the minimum value may be greater than the maximum value. A complaint from the GUI at this point would probably not be helpful, since the user is likely to enter a larger value for the maximum value.

SOLUTION

Form-based interactions are usually presented with text fields or other GUI components into which a user can enter information. The presentation also contains background label text that describes the information the user should enter into each field. It may also have additional title background text that is displayed in a prominent way and describes the interaction as a whole. One other mandatory element for form interactions is a way to indicate that the user has finished entering data. This usually takes the form of a push button with a caption such as "OK" or "Done."

If a form contains data entry GUI components that are not a text field, they usually consist of a radio button, list box, or other component that provides a selection interaction to choose a value for a piece of data. Such selection interactions usually constrain the possible values the user can specify to only valid values.

Arrange the GUI components in a grid-based pattern that is neat and visually guides the user's eyes through the elements in a logical order. Group closely related elements together.

Text fields in a form should do what they can to prevent users from entering invalid values. For example, if a text field is supposed to contain a number, the field could ignore any nonnumeric characters entered by a user.

Another way of helping users to enter valid values is to provide default values wherever appropriate. Where there is one value that is most common for a piece of data, providing the common value as a default simply improves the odds of obtaining the right value. In cases where there is no common value, a default value can be helpful for a different reason. If the type of information to be provided may not be obvious to a user, a default value can serve as an example of the requested information.

When it is not possible to prevent users from entering invalid values into a text field, it is desirable to immediately notify the user that there is a problem. However, because such notifications can cause problems, they are not usually given during form interactions. These problems are addressed by the Ephemeral Feedback pattern.

When the user indicates that he or she has finished entering data, the GUI should check that each of the entered values is valid and consistent with the other values. The GUI should also check that the user has provided all required data. If there are any invalid values, inconsistencies, or missing values, the GUI should notify the user of the problem.

If it is likely that users will be unfamiliar with a form, provide a visual indication of what data is required and what data is optional. This gives the user a better chance of getting it right on the first try.

CONSEQUENCES

- A program is able to obtain pieces of data from a GUI.
- The rest of the program is able to assume that the GUI has performed the validity and consistency tests for which it is responsible.

- The GUI gives the user guidance regarding the values that must be supplied and their validity.

IMPLEMENTATION

There are two common extensions to text-field components that are used to prevent invalid values from being entered into a text field. The first extension to a text-field class is to allow a *format mask* to be associated with its instances. A format mask is a string that specifies the format of what can appear in a text field. For example, the format string 000-00-0000 might indicate that the text field will always contain 11 characters, all of which are required to be digits, except the fourth and seventh, which are always a hyphen.

There is no standard interpretation of format masks. Each implementation defines its own interpretation. It is possible to define format masks for dates and other types of data. Text fields may use format masks to reject characters that are inconsistent with the mask and to determine the default characters that appear in otherwise uninitialized text fields.

The other type of extension to text fields is to associate a range of values with a text field. The idea is that text fields extended in this way should contain values in a specified range. They can refuse to accept characters that cause the contents of the text field to be out of range.

Whether these extensions should be used to quietly reject characters or detect invalid values depends on the type of users who will be using the GUI. Users who are not good typists are more likely to look at the screen as they type and notice if it does not show what they expect. Proficient touch typists do not normally look at the screen as they type, so quietly rejecting invalid keystrokes may result in entering incorrect data.

A GUI that implements a form interaction will usually pass the data it collects on to some types of data objects that throw an exception if the data violates their constraints. A GUI should pass any such complaints on to the user. Error messages generated in this manner are not always detailed enough for the user to under-

stand, nor is it always clear which fields the data object is refer-
encing. For this reason, the GUI should perform its own checking
on the validity and consistency of its data values. Ideally, the GUI
should be able to delegate checking the validity and consistency
of individual fields to the data object that is responsible for it.
When this is not possible, you must make a design tradeoff
between a GUI that produces good error messages and the additional effort that may be required to keep the GUI's validity
checking consistent with the data object's validity checking.

The purpose of most form interactions is either to collect
data or to edit previously collected data. When collecting data, it
can be helpful to include a cancel button in the GUI that aborts
the interaction. When editing data, it may be even more helpful
to have a reset button in the GUI that sets all of the values in the
GUI to the original values.

RELATED PATTERNS

Supplementary Window   Form interactions often occur within
a dialog.

Ephemeral Feedback   The Ephemeral Feedback pattern provides guidance in providing brief, short-lived feedback to a
user.

Explorable Interface   The Explorable Interface pattern
describes a technique for making a form interaction more useable.

Selection   Form interactions often include selection interactions to select data values.

Direct Manipulation [Grand99]

SYNOPSIS

Allow users to interact with objects by manipulating the representations of objects presented by a GUI.

CONTEXT

Suppose you work for a company that makes toy building blocks. The company's marketing department is responsible for creating large and impressive displays that are built from the blocks and sent to stores to attract customers. Currently, just a few master builders create original displays from the building blocks. Assistant builders then build the copies that are sent out to stores.

To accommodate the growing number of stores that carry the company's products, the company wants to be able to create displays more quickly without having to hire and train more assistant builders. The company would also like to produce a larger variety of displays.

The company has decided on a solution to these problems. The company wants to create a computer system that will allow all of its builders to build original virtual displays. The computer will then direct a robot arm to quickly and accurately build physical copies of the virtual displays.

Suppose it is your task to design the portion of this computer system's GUI that will allow builders to create virtual displays. You decide that the logical interaction style for this is *direct manipulation*.

Direct manipulation is a GUI interaction style that presents visual representations of objects to users, allows users to issue commands to manipulate the displayed objects, and then displays the results of the manipulation. For example, a file browser that supports direct manipulation might allow a file to be moved to another directory by dragging it and dropping it in the desired directory. After the drag and drop is done, the display is updated so that the file appears in its new directory and not in its original directory.

Some of the manipulation commands that you are likely to need for the building-block application include:

- Drag a block from a palette and place it in the display.
- Place multiple blocks in a row.
- Change the color of blocks that you have already placed.

Word processors and drawing programs are common applications that usually use a direct manipulation interaction style.

FORCES

- When using a program to manipulate objects, users need to know the current state of the objects and the effect of their manipulations. If the program does not provide this information, users have the burden of either maintaining a continuous mental model of the objects they are manipulating or frequently examining the objects to determine their current state.
- Displaying a representation of the objects a user is manipulating relieves the user of having to maintain a mental model of the state of those objects and the results of the manipulations.
- Suppose a program's GUI uses direct manipulation as its primary interaction style. If the objects it manipulates are concrete, and the ways the GUI offers to manipulate them are similar to the ways users manipulate corresponding real-world objects, then some users may need no documentation or training to use the GUI.
- When the GUI provides users with immediate visual feedback on the effects of commands, users can immediately recognize when the results of a command are not what they expected.

- A consistent way of applying commands to objects in the GUI's presentation, such as point and click or drag and drop, makes the GUI easier to learn. In particular, it supports an exploratory or trial-and-error approach to learning.
- You want to provide a way of interacting with a GUI that minimizes the opportunities for users to make errors in the way they enter commands.

SOLUTION

Have a GUI interact with users by presenting a visual representation of objects to be manipulated. Allow users to manipulate objects by pointing at the objects and gesturing with a pointing device. Ensure that the visual representation of objects reflects the most current manipulations.

CONSEQUENCES

- A direct manipulation style of interaction gives users the impression that they are in direct control of the objects presented to them by the GUI.
- Consistency between the presentation of objects and the actual objects is very important.
- Direct manipulation interactions are visual in nature and make it easy for users to use commands with which they are unfamiliar. Since most people are visually oriented and learn best through trial and error, GUIs based on direct manipulation are easy to learn.
- The highly visual nature of direct manipulation interactions makes it difficult for visually impaired people to work with them. Working with interactions based on conversational text is usually easier for visually impaired people.
- Direct manipulation interactions are more difficult to implement than other styles of interaction.
- Capturing and manipulating a command history from a direct manipulation is difficult. Reusable mechanisms do not

understand the commands in the context of the problem domain. Problem-specific mechanisms are generally not reusable. Saving history for later use as a macro is prone to problems arising from differences between the original context and the context in effect when the macro is invoked.

■ Many users find direct manipulation interactions to be more fun than other types of interactions.

IMPLEMENTATION

There are two commonly implemented mechanisms for directing the manipulation of objects in a direct manipulation interaction:

1. **Point and click.**   Point and click means that a user can manipulate an object by pointing at it, clicking on it to select it, and specifying a command. The user typically specifies the command through a pull-down menu. It can also be specified through keyboard shortcuts. Another form of shortcut is to click on the object to be manipulated in a way that causes a pop-up menu to appear and then select a command on that menu. Most GUIs respond with a pop-up menu if the user clicks with the rightmost mouse button. Pop-up menus should contain the most common commands that apply to the clicked object. Such commands usually include copy and move.

2. **Drag and drop.**   Drag and drop means that a user can manipulate an object by dragging it to an icon or button that represents the action to be performed on the object (i.e., copy, print, etc.). Drag and drop may be faster for most users. It does require greater manual dexterity than point and click. Drag and drop also requires more display area to accommodate the icons.

Point and click is the more common of the two mechanisms. Some GUIs implement both.

The GUI can present the user with many kinds of helpful feedback and clues about the context of a direct manipulation interaction. One such type of feedback is to vary the way that the mouse pointer is presented. For example, if the GUI expects that there will be a noticeable delay while it carries out a command, the mouse pointer will typically change to an hourglass, a watch, or some other timepiece. It is also important that the GUI gives this sort of feedback when the meaning of some mouse gestures changes depending on what the mouse is pointing at. For example, if the mouse pointer is over an object for which the default action is to move the object, the mouse pointer might assume the shape of a hand.

When the user is dragging an object on the screen, it is helpful to provide feedback showing the object being dragged. An obvious way to do this is to show the object moving as the mouse pointer moves. However, it turns out that this is not a good way to provide this feedback. Moving the entire object can be a problem because the entire object may obscure the place to which the user is moving the object. Instead, it is customary to show an object being moved by showing its outline or a small, partially transparent icon being moved in place of the whole object.

For similar reasons, GUIs normally present feedback on resize operations on an object by showing the object's outline.

An important consideration for some direct manipulation interactions is that the presentation of objects on the screen be as close as possible to the appearance of the objects when they are produced in a physical form. For example, it is very important that a word processor shows words on the screen exactly as they will appear when printed. This property of GUIs is called *what you see is what you get* (WYSIWYG).

Working entirely through pointing devices may be slower for experienced users than typing a sequence of keystrokes. Users should be able to issue direct manipulation commands from the keyboard as much as possible.

RELATED PATTERNS

Ephemeral Feedback   The Ephemeral Feedback pattern provides guidance in providing brief, short-lived feedback to a user.

Explorable Interface   The Explorable Interface pattern describes a technique for making a form interaction more useable.

Selection   The Selection pattern is used when a direct manipulation interaction that supports menus is used to select a command to manipulate previously selected objects.

Limited Selection Size [Grand99]

SYNOPSIS

Design the presentation of selection interactions to avoid displaying more than a limited number of choices at a time.

CONTEXT

Experience and usability testing have shown that when a selection interaction confronts a user with too many related items from which to choose, users slow down or become temporarily confused. Guidelines for designing user interfaces usually recommend a limit in the range of seven, plus or minus two, items to be displayed at once.

FORCES

- Displaying a large number of choices to a user during a selection interaction can slow or confuse the user.
- Limiting the number of choices displayed at one time to the user during a selection interaction can reduce the amount of confusion or uncertainty caused by a large number of choices. If the way the choices are displayed not only limits the number of choices displayed at once but also adds a visible structure to the choices, it will take the user less time to find the right choice.

  It is often possible to organize courses of action into static categories. Often the only static category that data can be made to fit is a static set of ranges. If this is not useful, the next best organization may be a natural ordering of the data, such as alphabetization.
- Unrelated choices may be presented in the same selection interaction. For example, a pop-up menu may contain

choices that relate to the object that was clicked (i.e., copy, delete, etc.) and to any other choices that relate to an entire set of objects (i.e., print, save, etc.). Unrelated choices that are presented together as if they were related choices can be more confusing than the same number of related choices.

SOLUTION

Avoid displaying more than a limited number of related choices at the same time during a selection interaction. A typical limit is seven. Many successful GUIs are designed with a limit as low as five or as high as nine.

If the purpose of a selection interaction is to choose a course of action, the number of choices presented to users at once is usually limited by using a hierarchical selection interaction, such as a cascading menu. If the purpose of a selection interaction is to select a data value, it is more common to present the data as a scrollable list ordered by a natural ordering of the data, such as alphabetization.

If a pull-down or pop-up menu has too many choices that are not all related, consider grouping the related choices together and adding dividers to separate unrelated choices. If the number of choices in each group is under the limit and the number of groups is under the limit, the result is usually satisfactory.

CONSEQUENCES

- Structuring selections so that they do not burden users with too many choices at a time allows users to find the choice that they are looking for more quickly.
- Excessive nesting of selections slows the user down.

IMPLEMENTATION

Many guidelines for designing GUIs recommend a maximum number of choices to present to a user at once. Though the specific recommendation varies with the guideline, the recommendations are all in the range of five to nine. Pick a limit in that range and use it consistently in GUIs that you design.

RELATED PATTERNS

Selection   The Limited Selection Size pattern provides guidance on designing the presentation of selection interactions.

Ephemeral Feedback [Grand99]

SYNOPSIS

Provide feedback to users about the status of their work, without interfering with the natural flow of their work.

CONTEXT

Immediate feedback about the progress, success, and failure of interactions the user has with the GUI can be very valuable in reassuring the user that all is well or in alerting the user that there is a problem. However, if the delivery of feedback interferes with the natural flow of the work, then the feedback itself may be a problem. For example, consider the following extreme case:

A user is entering data from paper forms into a GUI form that has 20 fields. The user has gotten into the rhythm of the work and is entering data from the paper forms without looking at the screen. Without realizing it, the user makes a mistake when entering the second field of a form. After the user finishes entering the contents of the second field, the GUI detects the error and puts up a modal dialog box that says there is a problem with the contents of the second field. The modal dialog box is designed to stay up until the user presses Enter or clicks on its OK button.

The user is looking at the paper form, not the screen, and does not see the dialog box. Instead, the user keeps on entering keystrokes, which the dialog box discards. After entering all the data on the form, the user looks at the screen and notices the dialog box. At that point the user presses Enter to get rid of the dialog box and reenters the data from the rest of the form.

In the preceding scenario, the GUI failed the user in two ways. First, it did not get the user's attention when the problem actually occurred. It then compounded that failure by discarding the user's keystrokes, which forced the user to enter the same data twice.

The feedback mechanism in this scenario would not have been a problem for an application where the user is expected to be looking at the screen. Poorly designed feedback mechanisms can interfere with the natural flow of a user's work even if the user is looking at the screen. Consider the following scenario:

A user is editing information in a form to reprogram an elevator in a hotel. Currently, the elevator is programmed to stop at floors 2 to 12. The user wants to change that range to floors 14 to 20. The user begins by changing the minimum floor from 2 to 14. When the user attempts to move on to the next field, the GUI pops up a dialog box saying that the minimum floor cannot be greater than the maximum floor. After a few minutes of bewilderment, the user realizes that to get past the message dialog, you have to change the maximum floor to 20 first, and then change the minimum floor to 14.

The first scenario would have had a better outcome if the GUI had somehow gotten the user's attention when it detected a problem. It could have accomplished this by producing an appropriate sound.

In both of these scenarios, the GUI provided immediate feedback, which is good. What is bad is that the GUI insisted that the user respond to the feedback immediately. If the GUI had produced the feedback without requiring an immediate response, there would have been no problem.

FORCES

- Users may benefit from immediate feedback about the status of their work.
- If the GUI provides immediate feedback to users, it should wait until the last possible moment before requiring users to respond to the feedback, if it requires any response at all.
- When the GUI provides the user with feedback that is of an urgent nature, it may be helpful for the GUI to get the user's attention by making a sound.
- For some types of GUIs, producing positive feedback in the form of sounds can encourage the user to use the program

and make the user feel more confident while using the program.

SOLUTION

It is good for a GUI to provide immediate feedback to users about the status of their work, provided that the feedback does not interfere with the natural workflow. Feedback that does not interfere with the flow of work is usually ephemeral in nature. If it is visual in nature, it will either be visible until the GUI replaces it with another feedback message or it may disappear after a set amount of time has elapsed.

Visual feedback that is ephemeral in nature should always be presented in the same area of a GUI, usually off to the side, to make it easier for users to find it. Such an area is typically called a *status bar* and holds only a single line of text.

When a program is processing a command and the user will be forced to wait for the completion of the command, it can be reassuring to users to see a progress indicator. Though the progress indicator may appear in the status bar, it is common for GUIs to present progress indicators in a more prominent position.

Audio feedback should last only as long as the natural length of the sound being produced. Repeating a sound simply to lengthen the amount of time that a user hears it will usually annoy users after a while.

Audible feedback that draws attention to problems may be helpful in a program where the user may not otherwise be paying enough attention to the GUI's visual display to notice a visual notification. Audible feedback that provides positive feedback should be carefully designed not to distract from the user's work. If the user's work is divided up into small tasks, then the ends of the tasks may be the best time to provide positive feedback. Audible feedback is best given at times when the user should be thinking about the GUI itself and not the program's problem domain.

CONSEQUENCES

- GUIs should postpone the presentation of modal dialogs to provide feedback until the latest possible time. Modal dialogs force the user to deal with a problem immediately. This can distract the user from his or her intended plan of action, which may include fixing the problem.
- Use of the Ephemeral Feedback pattern can produce GUIs that are more difficult for visually challenged or hearing-impaired people to use.
- When designing a GUI to provide audible feedback, you must be sensitive to the physical environment in which the GUI will be used. In a business environment, GUIs that produce sounds may disturb people who are not using the GUI but are close enough to hear the sounds. The problem is compounded when people using the same program can hear each other's audible feedback. One way to solve this problem is to ensure that only the user of the GUI can hear the sounds it makes.

  On the other hand, there are environments where the production of sounds that everyone can hear is considered beneficial. For example, arcade games are expected to produce sounds that are audible to people who are not playing the game, so the game will attract more players.

IMPLEMENTATION

Because audible feedback can be a problem for some user environments, GUIs that provide audible feedback should also provide a way to disable the audible feedback.

Disabled Irrelevant Things [Tidwell98]

SYNOPSIS

Hide or disable GUI elements that are not relevant in the current context.

CONTEXT

It is bad for a GUI to present users with surprises. If a command is not available, a GUI's pull-down and pop-up menus should not imply that it is available. For example, most word processors have a pull-down menu item to print the current document. When a word processor is not editing a document, it has nothing to print. In this circumstance, the program's GUI will present the print menu item in a manner that indicates that it is not available. GUIs typically present such menu items in a grayed-out manner.

FORCES

- If a command or resource is clearly irrelevant to the current task, the GUI should not make it available to the user. This relieves users who are unfamiliar with a program of the burden of recognizing what is relevant and what is not.
- If the presence of a GUI component appears to indicate that a command or resource is available and the user tries to use the command, the user will be surprised when it doesn't work.
- Displaying a menu item or other GUI component as disabled tells the user that the item is not currently available.
- Suppose that a command is not available in a program without obtaining an add-on or an additional license. In this case, the publisher of the program may not want the command to appear in any menu so that users do not wonder how to enable the command.

- Users may expect that there is something they can do to change a disabled GUI component into an enabled GUI component. If there is nothing users can do to enable an item, it may be best not to include the item in a menu. Users do not usually expect to enable what they cannot see.

SOLUTION

If a command or resource is available in a program, but not within the current context, the GUI component that advertises the existence of the command or resource should be displayed as disabled. If a command or resource is unavailable in a program and no direct action by a user will make it available, it should not appear in the GUI at all.

CONSEQUENCES

- GUI components do not imply that commands are enabled if they are not.
- GUI components do not imply that users can enable a command if they cannot.
- Users are not given the impression that they can do something that they cannot.

IMPLEMENTATION

Publishers sometimes decide, for business reasons, that they want commands that are unavailable without the purchase of an additional license to appear in menus so that users will inquire about the possibility of purchasing the additional license.

RELATED PATTERNS

Selection   The Disabled Irrelevant Things pattern is used with the Selection pattern.

Supplementary Window [Grand99]

This pattern is also known as *Dialog*.

SYNOPSIS

Display a window for a user interaction that supplements a parent window's interaction. The purpose of the supplementary window is to collect information for the parent window's interaction, display additional information about the parent window's interaction, or provide a notification about the status of the parent's interaction. The supplementary window is shorter lived than its parent.

CONTEXT

Standalone windows or frames usually have a specific purpose. The visual structure of a window usually reflects that purpose, with each portion of the window dedicated to the presentation of a specific type of information. If a window becomes involved in a user interaction that involves the presentation or collection of information that the window is not equipped for, it pops up a supplementary window called a *dialog*.

For example, suppose that a user asks a word processor to save a new document. If the new document does not already have a file name associated with it, then the word processor will need the name of the file in order to save the document. The word processor window that the user uses to edit the document should not include a way of directly asking the user for a file name, because that is not its function. Instead, it pops up a dialog that prompts the user for a file name.

FORCES

- A window or frame should be organized to perform a cohesive task. Supplementary tasks that cannot be incorporated into the window or frame without making it less cohesive should be the responsibility of a dialog.

- Some dialogs pop up to deliver an urgent notification that the user should see before continuing with the business of its parent window. To ensure that the user sees the notification before continuing, the user should be forced to close the dialog before being allowed to work with the parent window again. An example of such a notification would be that the file a user wants to work with cannot be found.

- Some dialogs pop up to collect information needed to complete an operation initiated by the dialog's parent. If the information is required before the operation can be completed, the operation must not continue until the user has supplied the information. An example of this is a dialog that gets the name of a file with which the user wants to work.

SOLUTION

When information must be presented to or collected from the user, and that interaction cannot be made a coherent part of the window that initiates it, then the interaction should occur in its own dialog.

All dialogs must provide a way for the user to indicate that he or she is finished with the dialog. Many dialogs accept no commands other than an indication that the user is finished interacting with the dialog. Because most dialogs accept only a few commands, it is customary for the commands offered to a user by a dialog to be presented as pushbuttons rather than as pull-down menus. If a dialog accepts more than seven commands, consider putting some of them in a pull-down menu. See the Limited Selection Size pattern for more guidance on this issue.

Some dialogs must prevent the user from interacting with the dialog's parent window until the user is finished interacting with the dialog. Dialogs that prevent the user from interacting with their parent are called *modal* dialogs.

CONSEQUENCES

- The set of interactions a window can initiate does not have to be coherent in order for the window to provide a coherent visual presentation of its primary interaction.
- Modal dialogs can ensure that interactions occur in a particular sequence.

IMPLEMENTATION

The major considerations when designing a dialog are:

- Determine the details of presenting the interaction to the user.
- Decide if the dialog will be modal.
- Determine which commands the dialog will accept and how it will present them as pushbuttons.

The rest of this section concerns the presentation of buttons in dialogs. The suggestions for button presentation are based on common practice.

Place buttons that affect the entire dialog in a single row on the bottom of the dialog or in a single column on the right side. Some white space should separate those buttons from the rest of the dialog. Figure 5.11 shows an example of a dialog box with buttons on the bottom. Figure 5.12 shows an example of a dialog with buttons on the right. Dialogs that have buttons in both places are unusual.

There are some common labels that appear on dialog buttons. Table 5.1 shows some common labels and their usual meanings.

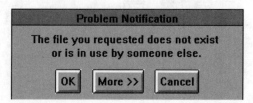

FIGURE 5.11 Problem notification dialog.

FIGURE 5.12 Password protection dialog.

You should determine a standard order in which the buttons will appear on the dialogs you design. If a dialog has an OK button, that button is customarily the first. If there is a Help button, that button usually appears last.

Place buttons that relate to only one part of a dialog in that part of the dialog. Figure 5.13 shows an example of a dialog that has a button that relates to only part of the dialog. In this dialog, the button labeled "Background . . ." is related to the Properties part of the dialog. It does not affect the course of the entire dialog in the way that the OK or Cancel buttons do. Something else to note about this button is that its caption ends with an ellipsis (. . .). It is common to put an ellipsis at the end of a button label to indicate that when the user presses the button another dialog will pop up to collect additional information from the user.

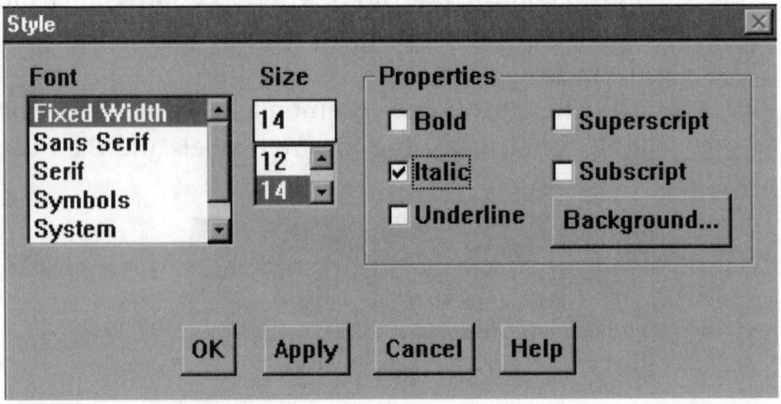

FIGURE 5.13 Style dialog.

TABLE 5.1 Common Labels and Meanings

Label	Meaning
OK	Buttons with this label represent a command that carries out the dialog's intention. If the purpose of the dialog is to notify the user of something, a button press indicates that the user has seen the notification and causes the dialog to disappear. If the purpose of the dialog is to collect information needed to complete an operation, a button press indicates that the provided information should be validated and the operation should be completed.
Cancel or Dismiss	Buttons with this label represent a command to abandon the dialog's intention. When the user presses a button with this label, the dialog disappears and aborts any operation that would normally be completed after the user presses the dialog's OK button.
Reset	Buttons with this label appear on some dialogs that collect information. They represent a command that resets the fields of the dialog to default values. If the purpose of the dialog is to edit information that a program already possesses, then when the user presses a button with this label, the dialog restores its fields to the values they contained when the dialog began offering values for editing.
Apply	Buttons with this label appear on some dialogs that collect information. When the user presses an Apply button, the operation for which the dialog supplies information completes as if the OK button had been pressed. However, the dialog remains present, ready to reinitiate the operation when the user presses its OK or Apply buttons.
Close or Done	A button with this label is used in place of Cancel to make a dialog go away when there is no operation to be continued or canceled. Such buttons are typically found on windows that provide a read-only view of data, such as a graph generated from a spreadsheet. When users are presented with a sequence of dialogs to guide them through a sequence of operations, such as installation steps, the last dialog in the sequence typically has a Close button instead of a Cancel button because there is nothing left to cancel.
Help	Buttons with this label represent a command that provides help on how to use the dialog.
Next	When dialogs occur in a sequence, they generally have a button with this label that the user can press to move on to the next dialog.
Back	When dialogs occur in a sequence, they generally have a button with this label that the user can press to return to the previous dialog.

continues

TABLE 5.1 *(Continued)*

Label	Meaning
Finish	When dialogs appear in a sequence for the purpose of collecting information for an operation, such as an installation, the last dialog in the sequence prior to the operation will typically have a button with the label Finish. When the user presses this button, the operation begins. Such a dialog is usually not the last in its sequence, as there is typically a dialog after the operation that provides information about the operation's completion.
More>>	When the user presses a button with this label, it causes the dialog to increase in size and display additional information or fields. After the user presses the button, its caption should change to <<Less.
<<Less	When the user presses a button with this label, it causes the dialog to decrease in size and display less information or fields. After the user presses the button, its caption should change to More>>.

RELATED PATTERNS

Limited Selection Size   Use the Limited Selection Size pattern to decide if a dialog will have pull-down menus.

Window per Task   The Supplementary Window pattern is partially motivated by the Window per Task pattern.

Step-by-Step Instructions [Tidwell98]

SYNOPSIS

Lead a user through the steps of a task where the GUI tells the user what to do next, rather than the user telling the GUI what to do next.

CONTEXT

Suppose you are designing a GUI for an airport kiosk that arriving travelers will use to retrieve information about hotels, restaurants, and points of interest around town. To get the desired information about a particular point of interest, users will have to provide specific information about what they are interested in and where they are interested in finding it.

Many of the people who use the kiosk will be first-time users. Most will not have used it often enough to become expert in its operation. Nearly all of the users will be unfamiliar with the area.

If a user is unfamiliar with an application and the problem domain that it addresses, it's usually difficult or even impossible for the user to guide the application through the performance of a task. For this reason, you decide to structure the user interface so that it walks the user through the task. For example, upon stepping up to the kiosk, the user sees the selection: Hotels, Restaurants, Theaters... . If the user selects Restaurants, the kiosk shows a map of the area and asks the user to touch a part of the map that is of interest. The kiosk then shows a selection of cuisine types available in and around that area and asks the user to touch those of interest. The kiosk then displays the map again, showing the corresponding restaurants. The user may then proceed with additional steps.

The point of this example is that the user never has to worry about figuring out the next step. The user always arrives at the next step by following instructions or choosing the next step from a selection the kiosk presents on its screen.

FORCES

- Users who are unfamiliar with a problem domain are unlikely to formulate a set of steps to accomplish a task within that problem domain.
- Users who are familiar with a problem domain are generally able to formulate sets of steps to accomplish tasks within that domain. However, if they are unfamiliar with the GUI, they may encounter difficulty and frustration when they try to use the GUI to direct a program through the task steps that they want to follow.
- Users may not want to expend the effort required to learn a problem domain or a GUI, especially when they deal with the problem domain infrequently and the GUI even less often.
- Users who lack confidence in their knowledge of a problem domain or GUI may be uncomfortable leading a computer program through the steps of a task.
- If the GUI is structured to guide the user through the steps of a task, it relieves the user of the burden of formulating the steps and of leading the program through them.

SOLUTION

Organize the GUI so it guides the user through the steps of a task one step at a time. Each step should include clear instructions.

The amount of input required from the user should be minimal in order to maintain the perception that the computer is guiding the user. For this reason, it is preferable that when input is required, it be accomplished as a simple and reasonably sized selection, rather than by asking the user to perform data entry.

The steps of a task may branch. This means that there may be more than one choice for some steps. When possible, the GUI should infer the next step from information the user has provided in the normal course of performing a previous step. If the user must be consulted to determine the next step, the GUI should provide the possible choices for the next step to the user as a selection.

The most common method of presenting the selection of a next step is with a few buttons. If the number of possible next steps is large, consider an alternate presentation, such as a list, or make the selection hierarchical.

Sometimes the nature of the application domain suggests an alternate way of presenting the selection of a next step. For example, suppose that the application is a tool to guide a technician through the repair of a mechanical device. The GUI may ask the technician to point at the part that appears to be defective on a diagram of the device. The GUI can infer the next step based on the part indicated.

In applications where the users are likely to be familiar with the problem domain, a graphical map of the task's steps can be presented off to the side or at the bottom. The purpose of the graphic is to give the user a sense of where he or she is in the task.

Following the Explorable Interface pattern, you may decide to provide a button or other GUI component that allows users to return to the previous step. If the application is a kiosk where users are likely to leave and arrive during any step, it may be better to provide a button that returns the GUI to the first step or its initial state.

CONSEQUENCES

- Using the Step-by-Step Instructions pattern relieves users of the burden of formulating a sequence of steps to perform a task or to guide a program through those steps.
- A step that requests the user to enter an excessive amount of information can intimidate the user. Such steps should be broken into multiple steps.
- Users may grow impatient if there are too many steps in the task. One way of handling this is to allow users to stop and

continue later from where they left off. However, this solution is not appropriate for all environments.

- Highly experienced users may not want to work through individual steps, and may grow impatient.

RELATED PATTERNS

Selection Implementations of the Step-by-Step Instructions pattern usually rely heavily on selection interactions to acquire information from users.

Supplementary Window Sometimes the Step-by-Step Instructions pattern is used to supplement a GUI that requires the user to lead the program through tasks. Wizards that are available in popular word processing and spreadsheet programs are an example. When the Step-by-Step Instructions pattern is used to design a supplementary GUI, it is usually in the context of a dialog.

Organizational Coding Patterns

The patterns in this chapter demonstrate how to organize your code in ways that make it easier to read and maintain. An underlying principle for many of these patterns is that simple code is easier to understand and is less likely to contain bugs.

Accessor Method Name [Grand99]

SYNOPSIS

Use names and signatures for accessor methods that are easy to read and conform to the JavaBeans specification.

CONTEXT

Good object-oriented design demands that classes encapsulate the representation of their attributes, requiring other classes to access those attributes through accessor methods. Code that calls an object's accessor methods is easier to read if the accessor methods follow consistent naming conventions and have consistent signatures. This level of consistency also makes it easier to write correct code.

The JavaBeans specification specifies a set of rules for the names and signatures of accessor methods that allows the `java.beans.Introspector` class to automatically discover a class's accessor methods. Though intended for accessor methods that correspond to the properties of beans, the naming rules set forth by the JavaBeans specification can be used for all accessor methods.

FORCES

- If the name of a class's method does not suggest the method's purpose, you must dig further into the method to determine its purpose. If your goal is to look at the class to determine its overall structure, digging into methods can pose a distraction.
- It's easy to read code that calls accessor methods if the methods are all consistently named so that their purpose is clear from their names. If the purpose of a method is obvious from its name and signature, then there is no need for some-

one reading the code to stop and look at the method's definition or documentation.

- If the signatures for accessor methods follow a consistent
  and predictable pattern, then programmers are less likely to
  make mistakes when they write calls to accessor methods.
- Names that follow a pattern that is understood only by the
  programmer who wrote them have limited use.
- The choice of a naming pattern or *naming convention* should
  not require long names. Many programmers resist typing the
  extra keystrokes that accompany long names.
- Objects that conform to the JavaBeans specification are
  widely used by programmers. The JavaBeans specification
  provides a consistent naming convention for accessor methods for beans-compliant classes. Since the convention is so
  widely known, the beans naming convention is a good naming convention for all classes.

SOLUTION

If a class has a `Foo` attribute, then a method to fetch the value
of the `Foo` attribute should be named `getFoo` and a method to set
the value of the `Foo` attribute should be named `setFoo`.

If the value of the `Foo` attribute is a scalar of type `Bar` then
the signature for its get should be:

```
Bar getFoo()
```

The signature for its set method should be:

```
void setFoo(Bar value)
```

If the type of an attribute is `boolean`, then it is usually
preferable to prefix it with "is" rather than "get" to form the name
of the method for fetching the attribute. For example, if the name
of an attribute is `mimsy`, then the signature of the method that
fetches that attribute would be:

```
boolean isMimsy()
```

The signature of the method that set that attribute would be:

```
void setMimsy(boolean value)
```

If the value of the `Foo` attribute is an array of type `Bar` then the signature of its method to fetch a reference to the entire array is:

```
Bar[] getFoo()
```

The signature of its method to fetch an individual element of the array should be:

```
Bar getFoo(int ndx)
```

The signature of its method to set value of the `Foo` attribute to a different array should be:

```
void setFoo(Bar[] value)
```

The signature of its method to set an individual element of the `Foo` array should be:

```
void setFoo(Bar[] value, int ndx)
```

Note that set methods do not return a result. If they need to complain about a value, they should throw an exception.

CONSEQUENCES

- Programmers can understand the purpose of accessor methods that conform to these rules without consulting the method's documentation or source code.
- Programmers can assume that any method that follows the naming conventions for accessor methods is very inexpensive to call, because this is usually the case. Such assumptions can be very expensive when they are wrong.

IMPLEMENTATION

Although the naming conventions specified in this pattern description are Java specific, using a consistent naming convention for accessor methods is applicable to most object-oriented languages.

JAVA API USAGE

The rules for naming accessor methods specified under the "Solution" heading for this pattern come from the JavaBeans specification.

CODE EXAMPLE

The following class defines some accessor methods that conform to the Java API rules.

```
class Square {
    private double size;

    public double getSize() {
        return size;
    } // getSize()

    public void setSize(double newSize) {
        if (newSize < 0) {
            String msg = Double.toString(newSize);
            throw new IllegalArgumentException(msg);
        } // if
        size = newSize;
    } // setSize(double)
    ...
} // class Square
```

RELATED PATTERNS

Intention Revealing Method   The Accessor Method Name pattern contains rules for naming all accessor methods. The Intention Revealing Method pattern contains suggestions for defining and naming individual methods.

Anonymous Adapter [Grand99]

SYNOPSIS

Use anonymous adapter objects to handle events. This simplifies the code and allows code that relates to the same event source to exist in the same part of the source code.

CONTEXT

If an object is coded so that it directly receives events from multiple other objects, its code may be more complicated and difficult to read than necessary. Consider the following listing:

```
class ActionDialogMgr implements ActionListener {
    private JButton OKButton;
    private JButton cancelButton;
    private JButton applyButton;
    ...
    ActionDialogMgr() {
        ...
        OKButton.addActionListener(this);
        cancelButton.addActionListener(this);
        applyButton.addActionListener(this);
    } // constructor()

    public void actionPerformed(ActionEvent evt) {
        Object eventSource = evt.getSource();
        if (eventSource == OKButton) {
            doIt();
            dialog.setVisible(false);
        } else if (eventSource == cancelButton) {
            dialog.setVisible(false);
        } else if (eventSource == applyButton) {
            doIt();
        } // if
    } // actionPerformed(ActionEvent)
    ...
} // class ActionDialogMgr
```

This listing shows a class whose instances receive action events from three different JButton objects. When any of those JButton objects want to send an action event, they call the ActionDialogMgr object's actionPerformed method. Because its actionPerformed method is responsible for handling events from three different objects, it is cluttered with a chain of if statements. Also, its logic is less cohesive and more difficult to understand than it would be if the method were responsible for handling events from only one object. The complexity of methods such as these increase linearly with the number of event sources for which they are responsible.

Another difficulty in understanding the ActionDialogMgr class is that the code that creates the buttons and the code that handles events from the buttons are located in two different places. The code that creates the buttons is located in the class's constructor. The code that handles events from the buttons is located in the actionPerformed method. It would be easier to understand if all of the code related to creating a button and handling its events were located in the same place.

A simpler and more scalable approach is to use anonymous adapter classes to handle events. The following listing shows the ActionDialogMgr class reworked to use that approach.

```
class ActionDialogMgr2 {
    private JButton OKButton;
    private JButton cancelButton;
    private JButton applyButton;
    ...
    ActionDialogMgr2() {
        ...
        OKButton = new JButton("OK");
        OKButton.addActionListener(new ActionListener() {
            public void actionPerformed(ActionEvent evt) {
                doIt();
                dialog.setVisible(false);
            } // actionPerformed(ActionEvent)
        });
        ...
        cancelButton.addActionListener(new ActionListener() {
            public void actionPerformed(ActionEvent evt) {
                dialog.setVisible(false);
            } // actionPerformed(ActionEvent)
        });
```

```
        ...
    } // constructor()
    ...
} // class ActionDialogMgr2
```

FORCES

- Methods that handle events from multiple sources are more complicated than methods that handle events from a single source.
- When the code for setting up an event source is near the code that handles events from that source, the code is easier for people to read and understand.
- You can use an adapter object to receive and handle events from event sources. The advantage to using adapter objects is that you can create a different adapter object to receive from each event source. If an adapter object receives events from only one object, then the adapter's event-handling method is not concerned with identifying the event source.
- To ensure that an adapter object receives events from only one object, it is not sufficient that the object which creates the adapter only registers it to receive events from one object. The adapter object must not be accessible by any other objects.
- Making an adapter class accessible by only the class that instantiates it helps to ensure that its instances are used only in the manner that is intended. This is because the fewer places from which the class is accessible, the fewer situations there will be for a programmer to use the class incorrectly.
- Private inner classes declared as members of their enclosing class are accessible to their enclosing class but not to outside classes. However, such classes can be accessed by any code in their enclosing class.
- Private inner classes declared within a method are accessible only within the same block of the method in which they are declared.
- Putting the definition of an inner class in the method that sets up its event source allows the code for setting up the event source and handling its events to be as close as possible.

- Adapter classes that handle events are usually very simple and short. Typically, they handle events by calling a method in the enclosing class.
- If an adapter class is used in one place only, it does not need to have a name. If an adapter class is very simple, giving it a name it does not need supplies someone reading the class with information that may only distract from the class's true purpose.

SOLUTION

Rather than have event-handling objects receive events directly, have them receive events indirectly through anonymous adapter classes.

The following listing shows a class whose instances are the direct recipient of its own events.

```
class MyClass implements FooListener {
    ...
        myEventSource.addFooListener(this);
    ...
    public void handleFoo(FooEvent evt) {
        ...
    } // handleFoo
} // class MyClass
```

Instead of directly registering themselves with event sources as event listeners, as shown in the preceding listing, objects should register instances of anonymous adapter classes to receive events on their behalf. The listing that follows illustrates this technique.

```
class MyClass {
    ...
        myEventSource.addFooListener(new FooListener() {
            public void handleFoo(FooEvent evt) {
                ...
            } // handleFoo(fooEvent)
        });
    ...
} // class MyClass
```

In this listing, the class registers an instance of an anonymous adapter class as a listener for `Foo` events from `myEvent-Source`. The definition of the anonymous class and the registration of its instances as event listeners can appear in the code right next to the rest of the code that creates and sets up the event source.

CONSEQUENCES

- The event-handling methods of an adapter object that are dedicated to a single event source can be free of any tests for the identity of the event source. Also, because the adapter's event-handling method only contains logic for handling events from a single source, it is simpler and more cohesive.
- Because the definition of the anonymous adapter class appears in the code that registers its instance as an event handler, the code to handle events from an object can be adjacent to the code that sets up the object.
- The use of anonymous adapter classes increases the number of classes in a program and may increase the number of objects that it creates. Both of these reduce performance, but not usually enough to notice.
- Some adapter classes must use state information to determine how to handle an event. If events from different sources require the same type of state-sensitive handling, then using a different adapter class for each event source results in code duplication.

RELATED PATTERNS

Adapter   The Anonymous Adapter pattern uses Adapter objects. The Adapter pattern is described in Volume 1.

Mediator   If handling events from multiple sources involves managing or using common or interrelated state information, the Mediator pattern described in Volume 1 provides a better way to handle the events.

Hashed Adapter Objects   The Hashed Adapter Objects pattern provides a more flexible way to manage event handlers than the Anonymous Adapters pattern.

Symbolic Constant Name [Grand99]

SYNOPSIS

Use symbolic names for constants. A meaningful name makes the purpose of the constant clear to someone reading the code. Symbolic names can also simplify maintenance.

CONTEXT

Consider the following piece of code:

```
private OutputStream out;
...
public void writeAction(int action) throws java.io.IOException {
    if (action <3 || action >11) {
        throw new IllegalArgumentException(String.valueOf(action));
    } // if
    switch (action) {
      case 6:
          out.write('T');
          break;
      case 9:
          out.write('U');
          break;
      case 10:
          out.write('P');
          break;
    } // switch
} // writeAction(int)
```

It is not possible to tell what the purpose of this piece of code is just by looking at it. All that you can really tell from reading the code is that if the value passed into the method is 6, 9, or 10, then it will write a byte that contains a particular value. The code contains no clues about what all of that means. Compare it to the following piece of code:

```
private OutputStream out;
// Actions
```

```
static final int MIN_ACTION     = 3;
...
static final int START_ACTION   = 6;
static final int PAUSE_ACTION   = 9;
static final int STOP_ACTION    = 10;
static final int MAX_ACTION     = 11;
...
// Command Byte Values
static final int START_COMMAND = 'T';
static final int PAUSE_COMMAND = 'U';
static final int STOP_COMMAND  = 'P';
...
public void writeAction(int action) throws java.io.IOException {
    if (action<MIN_ACTION || action>MAX_ACTION) {
        throw new IllegalArgumentException(String.valueOf(action));
    } // if
    switch (action) {
      case START_ACTION:
          out.write(START_COMMAND);
          break;
      case PAUSE_ACTION:
          out.write(PAUSE_COMMAND);
          break;
      case STOP_ACTION:
          out.write(STOP_COMMAND);
          break;
    } // switch
} // writeAction(int)
```

In this second version of the code, the symbolic constants in the case labels provide excellent insight into the purpose of each case label.

FORCES

- Literal constants such as 23 or XYZ are just values with no intrinsic meaning.
- If a name conveys a meaning and that name is associated with a value, then where the name represents the value, people reading the code are able to infer the meaning of the value.
- Using a name in place of a literal constant should not hide the fact that a constant value is used.
- To communicate to people that an identifier represents a constant and not a variable, you can use a naming conven-

tion that makes names of constants look different from names of variables.

- A common naming convention for constants is to make the letters of the name all uppercase, separating the words with underscores. Java inherited this convention from C/C++; it's widely known and is older than Java itself.

SOLUTION

Use meaningful, symbolic names to represent constants in code. Avoid using literal constants to directly represent constants in code.

Make it obvious to people reading the code that a name represents a constant by making all the letters in the name uppercase and separating words within the identifier with underscores. For example, instead of writing

```
return celsius*1.8 + 32;
```

write

```
final static double CONVERSION_FACTOR = 1.8;
...
return celsius * CONVERSION_FACTOR + 32;
```

CONSEQUENCES

- When meaningful, symbolic names are used to represent constants in code, people reading the code know the meaning of the constant.
- The use of symbolic names to represent constants can reduce the effort required for maintenance. If the value of a constant must be changed and a symbolic name is *consistently* used to represent the constant, then only the definition of the symbolic name has to be changed. If a symbolic name is not used to represent the constant, then a programmer has to find every occurrence of the constant and change it. If what are logically two different constants have the same value, it is easy for a programmer to change some values that should not be changed.

- It is entirely too easy for programmers to forget to uppercase names that represent constants. When programmers forget to use this naming convention, they obscure the name's meaning. Sometimes such mistakes find their way into a published API. When this happens, people are stuck with the misleading names for a long time. For example, the core Java API includes the class `java.awt.Color`. It defines a number of color constants with names like `red`, `brown`, and `white` that are all lowercase.

IMPLEMENTATION

The usual way to define symbolic names in Java is as final static variables.

Some constants are commonly represented as *literals* in Java programs. For example, the lowest valid index of an array is 0. It is very common to see a 0 in the heading of a statement to indicate the lowest index of an array. Because this practice is widespread, there is usually no confusion about the meaning of the 0 in that context.

If an object is used as the value of a symbolic name that is supposed to represent a constant, then the object should be immutable. Strings are a common example of immutable objects that often are used this way.

JAVA API USAGE

The class `java.awt.event.KeyEvent` defines a number of symbolic names for constants that represent different keystrokes. The symbolic names allow you to write understandable code that checks for specific keystrokes. Instead of writing

```
if (keyEvent.get KeyCode()==0x70)
```

to determine if the F1 key was pressed, you can write

```
if (keyEvent.getKeyCode()=KeyEvent.VK_F1)
```

RELATED PATTERNS

Immutable   The Immutable pattern found in Volume 1 describes other uses for immutable objects.

Switch   Code that uses the Switch pattern should also use the Symbolic Constant Name pattern.

Define Constants in Interfaces [Trost98]

SYNOPSIS

Avoid having to qualify symbolic constant names with the name of the class that defines them. Define them in an interface so that any class that implements the interface can use the symbolic names without any qualification.

CONTEXT

Source code that refers to constants defined in other classes must qualify the name of the constants with the name of the class that defines them. For example, consider the following code:

```
if (action<Action.MIN_ACTION || action>Action.MAX_ACTION) {
    throw new IllegalArgumentException(String.valueOf(action));
} // if
switch (action) {
  case Action.START_ACTION:
      out.write(Action.START_COMMAND);
      break;
  case Action.PAUSE_ACTION:
      out.write(Action.PAUSE_COMMAND);
      break;
  case Action.STOP_ACTION:
      out.write(Action.STOP_COMMAND);
      break;
} // switch
```

This listing shows symbolic constants used in comparisons and case labels. All of the symbolic constants are prefixed by the name of the class that defines them.

FORCES

- Having to qualify the constant with the name of the class that defines it distracts someone who is reading the code from the meaning of the code.

- Many programmers find that typing the class name before each constant is annoying. They feel it is an imposition to have to type a name that implies the intent of the constant, without also having to type the additional keystrokes to tell people where the name came from.
- If a class implements an interface, it inherits the constants that the interface defines. Because it inherits them, programmers can refer to the name of a constant defined in the interface without qualifying the constant with the name of the interface.
- Some people prefer to see uses of constants defined in interfaces qualified by their interface name. Unless a programmer is using a tool that will automatically insert the interface name, it is not possible to reconcile this with programmers who do not want to type the extra keystrokes.

SOLUTION

Define constants in an interface like this:

```
interface ActionIF {
    // Actions
    public static final int MIN_ACTION          = 3;
    public static final int ROTATE_LEFT_ACTION  = 3;
    public static final int ROTATE_RIGHT_ACTION = 4;
    public static final int WARM_UP_ACTION       = 5;
    public static final int START_ACTION         = 6;
    public static final int UP_ACTION            = 7;
    public static final int DOWN_ACTION          = 8;
    public static final int PAUSE_ACTION         = 9;
    public static final int STOP_ACTION          = 10;
    public static final int ALARM_ACTION         = 11;
    public static final int MAX_ACTION           = 11;

    // Command Byte Values
    public static final int START_COMMAND = 'T';
    public static final int PAUSE_COMMAND = 'U';
    public static final int STOP_COMMAND  = 'P';
} // interface ActionIF
```

If a class that uses these constants is declared to implement the interface, then the class can refer to the constants without qualification like this:

```
class InterfaceExample implements ActionIF {
    private OutputStream out;

    public void writeAction(int action) throws IOException {
        if (action<MIN_ACTION || action>MAX_ACTION) {
            String msg = String.valueOf(action);
            throw new IllegalArgumentException(msg);
        } // if
        switch (action) {
          case START_ACTION:
              out.write(START_COMMAND);
              break;
          case PAUSE_ACTION:
              out.write(PAUSE_COMMAND);
              break;
          case STOP_ACTION:
              out.write(STOP_COMMAND);
              break;
        } // switch
    } // writeAction(int)
} // class InterfaceExample
```

CONSEQUENCES

- If a class is declared to implement an interface, then the class can refer to variables declared by the interface without qualifying them, unless their name conflicts with a name that the class inherits from a superclass or another interface.
- If a constant's name is not qualified by the name of the interface that defines it, programmers may have to go to more trouble to find the definition of the constant, depending on the tools they are using.
- When a class implements an interface that defines constants, the .class file that a compiler produces for it includes the values of the interface's constants. Compilers do not include those values if a class merely refers to an interface and does not implement it. For this reason, the use of Define Constants in the Interface pattern can cause an increase in the size of the compiled version of a class.

JAVA API USAGE

The interface `java.awt.swing.SwingConstants` defines constants for use by classes that use the Swing package.

RELATED PATTERNS

Symbolic Constant Name   This pattern applies only to classes that use symbolic names for constants.

Switch [Grand99]

SYNOPSIS

Select a piece of code to execute from multiple alternatives based on an `int` data value using a `switch` statement.

CONTEXT

Suppose you have some code that consists of a chain of `if` statements like this:

```
if (action == ROTATE_LEFT_ACTION) {
    out.write(LEFT_COMMAND);
} else if (action == ROTATE_RIGHT_ACTION) {
    out.write(RIGHT_COMMAND);
} else if (action == WARM_UP_ACTION) {
    out.write(START_COMMAND);
    out.write(PAUSE_COMMAND);
} else if (action == START_ACTION) {
...
```

This code is readable. However, it can be made even more so by simplifying the code.

FORCES

- A `switch` statement can replace a chain of `if` statements if the boolean expression in all of the `if` statements tests the same `int` value for equality with a different constant.
- Because the equality tests performed by a `switch` statement are implicit, someone reading a program that contains a `switch` statement doesn't need to read through full-blown expressions. They can just look at the constants.
- Some `switch` statements are very long because they must account for a large number of cases. Some coding standards

recommend or require that methods remain under a certain length. If a `switch` statement exceeds that length all by itself, you will want to break it into smaller pieces. The only reasonable way to break a `switch` statement into smaller pieces is by using `if` statements to check for ranges of values.

■ It is a common mistake for programmers new to object-oriented design to use `switch` statements when polymorphic method calls would be more appropriate. Where appropriate, polymorphic method calls are less bug prone and are usually faster. The following guidelines can help:

1. If a `switch` statement is used to distinguish different kinds of objects, a polymorphic method call is generally a better implementation choice than a `switch` statement.

2. When there is an action to select based on the value of an integer, the implementation choice should depend on the nature of the integer. If the sole significance of the integer is to imply an action, it's best to use a polymorphic method call. This is performed with a set of classes that either extend a common superclass or implement a common interface. Each class encapsulates a different action in a method that is inherited from the interface or superclass and overridden. To indicate that you want an action performed, you provide the code that initiates the action with an object that encapsulates the action, rather than an integer that implies the action. The code then simply calls the object's method that performs the action.

3. When the integer is a product of a computation, it is usually quite reasonable to use a `switch` statement to select an action based on the integer.

4. When the integer does not come from an object, it is always appropriate to use a `switch` statement to determine the type of object to construct. For example, suppose a program has to read flat-file records that contain an integer record type field. It's appro-

priate to use a `switch` statement in this case to determine what kind of object to construct for encapsulating information in that record.

SOLUTION

When the next piece of code to execute is determined by verifying the equality of a given `int` value to a number of constants, use a `switch` statement. Here is what the code segment shown under the "Context" heading looks like with its chain of `if` statements rewritten as a `switch` statement.

```
switch (action) {
  case ROTATE_LEFT_ACTION:
      out.write(LEFT_COMMAND);
      break;
  case ROTATE_RIGHT_ACTION:
      out.write(RIGHT_COMMAND);
      break;
  case WARM_UP_ACTION:
      out.write(START_COMMAND);
      out.write(PAUSE_COMMAND);
      break;
  case START_ACTION:
      ...
```

CONSEQUENCES

- Because `switch` statements impart more structure to the selection of the next statement to execute than a chain of `if` statements, their intent is easier to understand.
- It is easier for someone reading the code to find the statements associated with a particular value, because the values are not buried in expressions.
- Most compilers are able to generate code for `switch` statements that directs the flow of control to the appropriate statements in a small, fixed number of instructions. Though it is possible for a compiler to do the same for an equivalent chain of `if` statements, some compilers may generate code that executes the `if` statements in sequence. This makes the time

required to direct the flow of the control to the appropriate statements proportional to the number of `if` statements.

JAVA API USAGE

The class `java.awt.EventQueue` has a method called `postEvent` that can be called to queue an event for later delivery. The method provides special processing for some types of events. It uses a `switch` statement to perform special processing based on event codes.

RELATED PATTERNS

Hashed Adapter Objects `Switch` statements associate `int` values with pieces of code. The Hashed Adapter Objects pattern associates objects with pieces of code.

Symbolic Constant Name Code that uses the Switch pattern should also use the Symbolic Constant Name pattern.

Polymorphism In many situations, polymorphic method calls are a more appropriate technique than `switch` statements. However, people with a background in procedural programming who are new to object-oriented techniques often use `switch` statements when polymorphic method calls would be more appropriate.

Extend Super [Beck97]

SYNOPSIS

Implement a method that modifies the behavior of a superclass's method by calling the superclass's method.

CONTEXT

Suppose you want to ensure that a dialog is always on top of all other windows when it is made visible. You can implement that behavior by overriding the `setVisible` method that it inherits in order to extend the behavior of the inherited method like this:

```
public void setVisible(boolean b) {
    super.setVisible(b);
    if (b)
      toFront();
} // setVisible(boolean)
```

FORCES

- You want to override a method in a way that extends rather than replaces the behavior of the inherited method.
- The additional behavior will occur before and/or after the behavior of the superclass's method. It will not occur during the behavior of the superclass's method.
- The superclass does not have any hooks or other provisions for extending its behavior in the desired way and you cannot modify it in that way.
- You want to extend the superclass's behavior in the simplest possible way.
- Making a method rely on a superclass's method creates a dependency that may increase the maintenance cost of the class and its superclass over their lifetimes.

SOLUTION

To override a method named foo in a way that extends rather than replaces the behavior of the inherited method, use the construct super.foo() to have the overriding foo method call the overridden foo method.

The call to the overridden method usually occurs near the beginning or end of the overriding method.

CONSEQUENCES

- Implementing a class to call its superclass's methods is a perfectly reasonable thing to do. However, it does create a dependency between a class and its superclass. If the behavior of the superclass is stable, this is generally not a problem.
- It is important to be aware of the dependency to avoid a change to the behavior of the superclass that breaks its subclasses. If you control the superclass and have access to its source, then you should put a comment in the overridden method to alert programmers who maintain the code of the dependency. If the superclass comes from a third party, be careful to rely only on explicitly documented behavior.
- The Extend Super pattern is usually used to prolong the behavior of methods that were not designed specifically to be extended. This can sometimes result in subtle bugs when the code that extends the behavior uses a resource in a way that conflicts with the use of the resource by the superclass's implementation.

JAVA API USAGE

The java.io.LineNumberReader class has a method named read. Its read method extends the behavior of its superclass's read method by adding counting logic to keep track of the current line number.

RELATED PATTERNS

Composed Method   The Composed Method pattern describes the more general case of composing the behavior of a method from the behavior of other methods.

Template Method   The Template Method pattern described in Volume 1 provides a way to design a class that plans for its behavior to be extended by a subclass's methods. It provides more flexibility and control over how a subclass extends the behavior of its superclass than the Extend Super pattern at the expense of greater complexity. In particular, the Template Method pattern allows behavior of a subclass to occur in the middle of the execution of the superclass's methods. The Template Method pattern can also be used to force a subclass to extend a superclass in predefined ways.

Intention Revealing Method [Beck97]

SYNOPSIS

If the intention of a call to a general-purpose method is not obvious, define a method with a meaningful name to call the general-purpose method.

CONTEXT

Consider the following line of code:

```
if (LOCK_FILE.createNewFile()) {
```

Looking at this line of code, you decide that its meaning is not clear enough. You change the line to read:

```
if (CreateLockFile ()) {
```

You also define the method `CreateLockFile` like this:

```
/**
 * Create the lock file if it does not already exist.
 * @return true if the file was created;
 *         false if it already existed.
 */
private boolean CreateLockFile () {
   return LOCK_FILE.createNewFile();
} // CreateLockFile ()
```

FORCES

- The intention of a call to a general-purpose method is not always self-evident, especially if the method is called for its side effect. If a general-purpose method is called for the purpose of returning an object, the name of the variable to which the object is assigned can provide enough of a clue about its purpose.

- If the meaning of a line of code is not obvious, you can make its meaning clearer by writing comments. However, many programmers do not like to read or write comments. Therefore, the meaning of code should be as clear as possible without comments.

SOLUTION

Define a method with a meaningful name to call a general-purpose method. Replace the call to the general purpose method in the class's other methods with a call to the new method.

CONSEQUENCES

- The meaning of the call to the general-purpose method is easier to understand.
- The implementation of the operation encapsulated by the intention revealing method is less accessible. Instead of it appearing in line, someone reading the code has to flip to the definition of the method to see its implementation.

JAVA API USAGE

The class `java.awt.EventQueue` contains a statement that reads:

```
if (eventQueueListener != null)
  eventQueueListener.eventPosted(theEvent);
```

The meaning of this statement is not obvious. The class wraps the statement in a method with a meaningful name:

```
protected void notifyEventQueueListeners(AWTEvent theEvent) {
    if (eventQueueListener != null)
      eventQueueListener.eventPosted(theEvent);
```

RELATED PATTERNS

Composed Method   The Composed Method pattern provides other reasons for moving code into a separate method.

Composed Method [Beck97]

SYNOPSIS

Reorganize methods that are too large to easily understand into smaller methods.

CONTEXT

Consider the following lengthy piece of code:

```
LongDialog(Frame parent) {
    super(parent, "Banquet Room Reservation");
    BanquetMediator mediator = new BanquetMediator();
    Container contentPane = getContentPane();

    FlowLayout flowLayout;
    flowLayout= new FlowLayout(FlowLayout.CENTER, 20, 5);
    JPanel dispositionPanel = new JPanel(flowLayout);
    JButton okButton = new JButton("OK");
    mediator.registerOkButton(okButton);
    dispositionPanel.add(okButton);
    JButton cancelButton = new JButton("Cancel");
    dispositionPanel.add(cancelButton);
    contentPane.add(dispositionPanel, BorderLayout.SOUTH);

    JPanel bodyPanel = new JPanel(new BorderLayout(5,5));
    bodyPanel.add(new JSeparator(), BorderLayout.NORTH);
    JPanel mainPanel;
    mainPanel= new JPanel(new BorderLayout(5,3));
    mainPanel.add(createDateTimePanel(mediator),
                BorderLayout.WEST);
    mainPanel.add(createServicePanel(mediator),
                BorderLayout.CENTER);
    String foods[]= { "Roast Beef", "Egg Rolls", "Shish Kebob",
                "Burritos", "Lasagna", "Ham", "Veal Marsala",
                "Saurbraten", "Beef Wellington",
                "Mesquite Chicken"};
    JList foodList = new JList(foods);
    int mode = ListSelectionModel.MULTIPLE_INTERVAL_SELECTION;
    foodList.setSelectionMode(mode);
    foodList.setVisibleRowCount(7);
    mediator.registerFoodList(foodList);
```

```
    mainPanel.add(foodList, BorderLayout.EAST);
    bodyPanel.add(mainPanel, BorderLayout.CENTER);
    bodyPanel.add(new JSeparator(), BorderLayout.SOUTH);
    contentPane.add(bodyPanel, BorderLayout.CENTER);

    JPanel topPanel = new JPanel(new BorderLayout(10, 5));
    JPanel countPanel;
    countPanel = new JPanel();
    countPanel.add(new JLabel("Number of People (25-1600):"));
    JTextField countField = new JTextField(4);
    mediator.registerPeopleCountField(countField);
    countPanel.add(countField);
    topPanel.add(countPanel, BorderLayout.WEST);
    contentPane.add(topPanel, BorderLayout.NORTH);
    pack();
} // constructor(Frame)
```

This listing shows a constructor that contains most of the code that builds the contents of a dialog. The code is too long for someone reading the code to understand quickly. The following listing shows code that performs the same function but is broken down into smaller, easier-to-understand methods.

```
BanquetReservationDialog(Frame parent) {
    super(parent, "Banquet Room Reservation");
    BanquetMediator mediator = new BanquetMediator();
    Container contentPane = getContentPane();
    contentPane.add(createDispositionPanel(mediator),
                    BorderLayout.SOUTH);
    contentPane.add(createBodyPanel(mediator),
                    BorderLayout.CENTER);
    contentPane.add(createTopPanel(mediator), BorderLayout.NORTH);
    pack();
} // constructor(Frame)

// create panel with OK and Cancel Buttons
private JPanel createDispositionPanel(BanquetMediator mediator) {
    JPanel p;
    p = new JPanel(new FlowLayout(FlowLayout.CENTER, 20, 5));
    JButton okButton = new JButton("OK");
    mediator.registerOkButton(okButton);
    p.add(okButton);
    JButton cancelButton = new JButton("Cancel");
    p.add(cancelButton);
    return p;
} // createDispositionPanel()

// create top panel
private JPanel createTopPanel(BanquetMediator mediator) {
```

```
        JPanel top = new JPanel(new BorderLayout(10, 5));
        JPanel countPanel;
        countPanel = new JPanel();
        countPanel.add(new JLabel("Number of People (25-1600):"));
        JTextField countField = new JTextField(4);
        mediator.registerPeopleCountField(countField);
        countPanel.add(countField);
        top.add(countPanel, BorderLayout.WEST);

        return top;
    } // createTopPanel()

    // create panel that will be the body of the dialog
    private JPanel createBodyPanel(BanquetMediator mediator) {
        JPanel bodyPanel = new JPanel(new BorderLayout(5,5));
        bodyPanel.add(new JSeparator(), BorderLayout.NORTH);
        bodyPanel.add(createMainPanel(mediator), BorderLayout.CENTER);
        bodyPanel.add(new JSeparator(), BorderLayout.SOUTH);
        return bodyPanel;
    } // createBodyPanel()

    // create main panel that allows selection of the banquet details
    private Container createMainPanel(BanquetMediator mediator) {
        JPanel mainPanel;
        mainPanel= new JPanel(new BorderLayout(5,3));
        mainPanel.add(createDateTimePanel(mediator),
                    BorderLayout.WEST);
        mainPanel.add(createServicePanel(mediator),
                    BorderLayout.CENTER);
        String foods[]= { "Roast Beef", "Egg Rolls", "Shish Kebob",
                    "Burritos", "Lasagna", "Ham", "Veal Marsala",
                    "Saurbraten", "Beef Wellington",
                    "Mesquite Chicken"};
        JList foodList = new JList(foods);
        int mode = ListSelectionModel.MULTIPLE_INTERVAL_SELECTION;
        foodList.setSelectionMode(mode);
        foodList.setVisibleRowCount(7);
        mediator.registerFoodList(foodList);
        mainPanel.add(foodList, BorderLayout.EAST);

        return mainPanel;
    } // createMainPanel()
```

FORCES

- When methods are very short in length, it is very easy for someone to understand their purpose because the human mind is able to keep track of only a small number of things at one time.

- A large method can be broken down into multiple smaller methods.
- Classes written as many small methods are less buggy than classes written as a few large methods. Writing classes this way organizes the many statements that would have been in a single method into conceptually related groups of statements with names. The pieces are easier for the programmer to keep track of because outside of the method that the programmer is writing, he or she can think of the other pieces at the method level. This means having to think about fewer pieces than having to think about many individual statements when writing a single large method.
- In addition, larger methods are likely to have more local variables, which makes more interdependencies between statements possible. This makes bugs possible that are not possible when the statements are in different methods.
- If you are trying to understand the implementation logic of a method at its lowest level, it is more difficult to trace the logic of a method that has been organized into many submethods. It requires flipping between the method and its many submethods while mentally pushing and popping the many contexts.
- It is possible to carry the splitting of methods into smaller methods too far. If a method consists of just a few lines of code that are easily understood as a whole, splitting the method into smaller methods may not improve the ease of understanding the class to which it belongs. If the resulting methods are so small that their purpose is not clear, the class will be more difficult to understand.

SOLUTION

As you write the methods that are specified in an object-oriented design, break them into multiple methods that are called by the original method if you see that they are getting too large. Give each of the submethods a meaningful name to make it easier to understand the code. The submethods should be private, since there is not normally any reason to expose them to other classes.

If the implementation of a method includes distinct concepts or actions, it is usually best to organize the submethods so that they correspond to the concepts or actions of the original method.

CONSEQUENCES

- People can more easily understand classes that are organized into small methods.
- Methods that are small enough to be immediately understood are much less likely to contain bugs than are larger methods.
- Classes composed of small methods cost less to maintain. There are few bugs to fix, and small methods are usually easier to modify than larger methods.
- The object-oriented design that precedes writing classes can ensure that a program is well structured at the class level. Object-oriented design does not help much with designing the internal organization of a class's implementation. In the course of splitting large methods into smaller methods you may discover abstractions that you can use to better organize your implementation. You may also discover that some of the smaller private methods are reusable within the class.
- Sometimes, after applying the Composed Method pattern, you find yourself with a class that contains an unwieldy large number of small methods. This is often an indicator that the class should be split into multiple classes, with the original class acting as a façade for the additional classes (see the Façade pattern in Volume 1).

IMPLEMENTATION

There is no specific number of lines of code that is a hard limit on the length of a method. Reasonable lengths vary with coding style and the density of comments. A commonly used guideline is that methods should be small enough to be visible all at once within your editor's window. You can think of this as the *vertical guideline.* There is also a *horizontal guideline:* If the level of nested constructs in a method results in enough indentation that lines wrap or exceed the width of your editor window, consider splitting some level of the nesting into a separate method.

Methods that contain large `switch` statements or long chains of `if` statements should be allowed to exceed the length specified by whatever guideline you use for the maximum.

Many people are reluctant to adopt the practice of organizing classes into many small methods because they are concerned that it will result in inefficient code. In practice, this is rarely a problem. Many compilers are able to optimize such inefficiencies away. Most are able to merge the code of a called method back into its caller if the called method is private.

RELATED PATTERNS

Intention Revealing Method   The type of methods described by the Intention Revealing Method pattern should be the smallest methods that you create when applying the Composed Method pattern.

Maximize Privacy   The Maximize Privacy pattern provides the motivation for making submethods that are created by applying the Composed Method pattern private.

Façade   After applying the Composed Method pattern, you may decide to break a class up into smaller classes with the original class acting as a façade. The Façade pattern is described in Volume 1.

Conditional Compilation [Grand99]

SYNOPSIS

Control whether a compiler includes statements for debugging in the byte codes it generates or ignores those statements.

CONTEXT

To facilitate debugging, it is common to insert code into classes to trace the progress of a program or to check assertions. One way to manage this is to manually insert the debug code when you need it, and remove it when you are done. A better way to do this is to make the inclusion of your debug code conditional on a variable that you define. This way, you can turn the debug statements off and on by changing the value of a single variable.

FORCES

- You want to put debug code in your classes and turn the debug code on and off with a minimal amount of effort.
- If the only way to disable debug code is to physically remove it from the source, there is the possibility that code could be put into production with some active debug code if a programmer forgets to remove it.
- By making debug statements conditional on the value of a boolean constant, you control whether compilers will compile or ignore the debug statement.
- If the boolean expression at the beginning of an `if` statement is a constant, most compilers will treat the `if` statement specially. If the constant is true, most compilers that do any optimization will not generate any byte codes to test the value of the true constant. If the constant is false, the Java

language specification requires compilers to recognize that the statement will never be executed. The language specification also suggests that compilers not generate any byte codes for the `if` statement or the statement that it controls.*

- As of the time of this writing, at least one popular Java development environment includes a compiler that lacks special treatment for `if` statements with constant boolean expressions as mandated by the language specification. The use of such compilers with debug code can hurt performance.

SOLUTION

Control whether debug code is executed by using `if` statements that test the value of a boolean constant.

It is more convenient if the constants for controlling different kinds of debug statements are all defined in the same class. The following listing shows a class that defines constants that control debug statements for tracing the progress of a program and checking for assertions.

```
public class Debug {
    public static final boolean TRACE=true;
    public static final boolean ASSERTION_CHECKING=true;
    /**
     * This method sends a message to standard error if the
     * given assertion is false.
     * @param ok This is the assertion. If it is true, nothing
     *              happens. If it is false, a message is printed.
     * @param errMsg this message prints if the assertion is false.
     */
    public static final void assert(boolean ok, String errMsg) {
        if (!ok) {
            System.err.println(errMsg);
        } // if
    } // assert(boolean, String)
}
```

---

* James Gosling, Bill Joy, and Guy Steele. *Java Language Specification*. Addison-Wesley.

You can use the constants to control `if` statements that determine whether the debug statements are executed. The following listing shows an example of this.

```
public class Test {
    private static final int BUFFER_LENGTH = 100000;
    private byte[] buffer = new byte[BUFFER_LENGTH];

    /**
     * Read a file and return its checksum.
     * @param fileName the name of the file.
     * @exception IOException if there is a problem while
     *                        reading the file.
     */
    public long getChecksum(String fileName) throws IOException {
        if (Debug.TRACE) {
            System.out.println("Computing checksum");
        } // TRACE
        if (Debug.ASSERTION_CHECKING) {
            Debug.assert(fileName.length() > 0,
                         "file name is empty");
        } // ASSERTION_CHECKING
        FileInputStream fin = new FileInputStream(fileName);
        CheckedInputStream cin;
        cin = new CheckedInputStream(fin, new CRC32());
        while( cin.read(buffer, 0, BUFFER_LENGTH) != -1);
        if (Debug.TRACE) {
            System.out.println("Done computing checksum");
        } // TRACE
        return cin.getChecksum().getValue();
    } // getChecksum(String)
} // class Test
```

CONSEQUENCES

- By controlling the execution of `if` statements with the value of constants, you are able to reuse the `if` statements rather than having to edit them out when you don't need them.
- Most compilers evaluate `if` statements that are conditional on a constant at compile time. Therefore, they either generate or do not generate code for the statement controlled by the `if` statement. They don't generate code to test the constant, so there is no runtime overhead.

■ Inserting debug code into the middle of regular code can
make the regular code more difficult to read, because the
debug code interrupts the logic of the regular code.

IMPLEMENTATION

You should determine if your Java compiler provides special
treatment for if statements with constant boolean expressions as
required by the language specification. To do this, you can use
the javap tool that is included in the JDK or use a decompiler to
examine your compiler's output.

Some Java compilers will not optimize out the condition or
body of an if statement unless you specify a compiler option to
turn on optimization.

RELATED PATTERNS

Assertion Testing The Conditional Compilation pattern is
often used with the Assertion Testing pattern.

White Box Testing The Conditional Compilation pattern is
often used with the White Box Testing pattern.

Checked versus Unchecked Exceptions [Grand99]

SYNOPSIS

As part of its contract with its callers, a method can be expected to throw exceptions under certain circumstances. These exceptions should be checked exceptions. Any exceptions thrown by a method that are outside of its contract, such as exceptions to indicate internal errors or to help with debugging, should be unchecked exceptions.

CONTEXT

Most of the exceptions available for Java methods to throw are *checked exceptions*. If a checked exception can be thrown from within a method, the method is required to either catch the exception or declare that it throws the exception.

All exceptions are checked exceptions, unless they are an instance of `RuntimeException`, `Error`, or one of their subclasses. Such exceptions are unchecked exceptions. There is no requirement for callers of a method that throws an unchecked exception to catch the unchecked exception or declare that they throw it.

Instances of subclasses of `Error` are used to indicate a problem within the Java virtual machine, such as being out of memory or having a `.class` file that is incorrectly formatted. Instances of subclasses of `RuntimeException` are used to report errors in common low-level operations, such as integer division by zero or an out-of-range array subscript.

Suppose you're writing a method that can be called only on certain days of the week. If it is called on the wrong day of the week, you want it to inform its caller by throwing an exception. Looking at the exceptions included in the core Java API, you don't see an appropriate exception for this purpose, so you decide to define your own.

You decide to call the exception class `WrongDayOfWeek-Exception`. Another decision you will have to make about this class is what its superclass will be. You decide it is a choice between making it a subclass of `Exception`, to indicate that the exception is a checked exception, or making it a subclass of `RunTimeException`, to indicate that the exception is an unchecked exception.

Because you want programmers who write calls to your method to think about how their code will handle a `WrongDay-OfWeekException`, you decide to make it a checked exception and have `Exception` as its immediate superclass.

FORCES

- If a method can throw a checked exception, programmers who write calls to the method are forced to give some small amount of thought to how the exception will be handled. If they neither write a `try` statement to catch the exception nor declare that the calling method throws the exception, their Java compiler will issue an error message.
- Checked exceptions declared in a method's `throws` clause are part of the method's contract with its callers. A calling method is required to catch or declare that it throws the checked exceptions of the methods it calls. A method that overrides another method is not allowed to throw any checked exceptions that the overridden method does not throw.
- If a method throws an exception for a reason that is not based on its contract with its callers, the exception should be an unchecked exception. Methods are never required to catch or declare that they throw an unchecked exception. A method does not force its callers to take any responsibility for a condition by throwing an unchecked exception.
- It is common for debug code to be concerned with violations of the contract between a method and its caller.

SOLUTION

Do not write classes that are a direct or indirect subclass of `RuntimeException` or `Error`. You should never write a method that deliberately throws an unchecked exception. The exception to this rule is code for debugging or assertion checking.

If debug code works by throwing exceptions, it should throw unchecked exceptions. The actions of debug code are not part of any method's contract with its callers. Therefore, it is not appropriate for debug code to throw a checked exception unless the exception is supposed to be recognized by the method's callers as an exception that is part of the method's expected actions.

Similarly, it is often appropriate for assertion-checking code that verifies that a method's callers are living up to their contract to throw unchecked exceptions, such as `IllegalArgumentException` or `IllegalStateException`.

Throwing a checked exception is appropriate under conditions when you want a method's callers to take responsibility, but under which they cannot reasonably check themselves. For example, suppose that an object encapsulates a communications link. A call to one of its methods that tries to read or write data through the communication link throws an exception if the link is not ready for use. It is not always possible for the method's caller to know in advance that the link is not ready. Making it throw a checked exception under these conditions ensures that a calling method deals with the problem after the call.

CONSEQUENCES

- A correctly functioning bug-free program should never throw an unchecked exception. This means that you can use unchecked exceptions to help with debugging.
- Unchecked exceptions thrown by debug code will not inadvertently be mistaken for an exception that is thrown during normal operation. There is no need to modify code to accommodate unchecked exceptions thrown by debug code.

- If debug code throws a checked exception that is outside the contract its method has with its callers, then its method and its method's callers will need to be modified when inserting or removing the debug code. Besides being extra work, code modification can introduce new bugs. For these reasons, debug code should never throw any checked exceptions that are not part of its method's contract with its callers.
- By specifying methods so that their contracts with their callers include only checked exceptions, you can rely on the semantics of Java to ensure that the callers deal with the exceptions.

JAVA API USAGE

Classes that implement the interface `java.util.Iterator` have methods named `next`, `hasNext`, and `remove`. If the `next` method is called when the `Iterator` object has no next element, the `next` method should throw the unchecked exception `NoSuchElement-Exception`. Calling the `next` method when the `Iterator` object has no next element is a programming error because the caller is supposed to first call the `hasNext` method to find out if there is a next element.

CODE EXAMPLE

The class that follows defines an exception class named `AssertionException`.

```
public class AssertionException extends RuntimeException {
    public AssertionException(String msg) {
        super(msg);
    } // class AssertionException
} // class AssertionException
```

This exception class is an unchecked exception because it is a subclass of `RuntimeException`. Because it is unchecked, methods that throw an `AssertionException` do not have to declare so. The following example shows such a method that throws `AssertionException`.

```
public static final void assert(boolean ok, String errMsg) {
    if (!ok) {
        System.err.println(errMsg);
        throw new AssertionException(errMsg);
    } // if
} // assert(boolean, String)
```

RELATED PATTERNS

Assertion Testing   The Assertion Testing pattern provides additional guidance about checked or unchecked exceptions to report unsatisfied assertions.

Conditional Compilation   The Conditional Compilation pattern can be used to prevent debug code that throws unchecked exceptions from being included in a production version of a class.

Convert Exceptions [Brown98]

SYNOPSIS

Many programs are organized into layers related to different domains, such as a database management domain and an application domain. In such programs, some classes are part of one domain but have methods that call methods of classes that belong to another domain. Such methods should convert exceptions they do not handle from the other domain to their own domain.

CONTEXT

Suppose you are writing an application. The application uses a number of classes to implement its commands. Each of those classes defines a method to implement a command. Some of those methods throw an exception if there is a problem in executing the command for which the method is responsible. To keep the application simple, you don't want it to have to handle many different exceptions being thrown by its commands. For this reason, you decide that all command implementing classes will be required to implement this interface:

```
public interface CommandIF {
    public void execute(String arg) throws ApplicationException;
} // interface CommandIF
```

By insisting that all command-implementing classes implement the CommandIF interface, you ensure that the only checked exception their execute methods can throw is ApplicationException, which is a class you have defined for this application.

Suppose the application you are writing will have a command to extend itself by loading classes that implement additional commands. To load these classes, the execute method that implements this command calls the Class class's forName method. If the forName method is unable to load a class, it throws a ClassNotFoundException.

Even though a ClassNotFoundException is thrown from within the execute method, the execute method may throw only an ApplicationException. To accomplish this, the execute method must catch any ClassNotFoundException thrown from within itself and handle it by throwing an ApplicationException, like this:

```
public class LoadCommand implements CommandIF {
    public void execute(String arg)
                throws ApplicationException {
        Class commandClass;
        try {
            commandClass = Class.forName(arg);
        } catch (ClassNotFoundException e) {
            String msg = "Unable to load command";
            throw new ApplicationException(msg, e);
        } // try
        ...
    } // execute()
} // class LoadCommand
```

Notice that the constructor for ApplicationException takes two arguments. The first argument is the usual message that is passed into constructors of message objects. The second argument is the ClassNotFoundException that was thrown. The ApplicationException class has a method to allow code that catches ApplicationException to retrieve the original exception. It also delegates printStackTrace operations to the original exception so that the stack trace reflects the location of the original problem.

Here is a listing of the ApplicationException class:

```
public class ApplicationException extends Exception {
    private Throwable exception; // The exception that gave
                                 // rise to this.
    /**
     * Constructor
     * @param msg Why this exception was thrown.
     */
    public ApplicationException(String msg) {
```

```
        super(msg);
    } // constructor(String)

    /**
     * Constructor
     * @param A description of why this exception was thrown.
     * @param The exception that gave rise to this exception.
     */
    public ApplicationException(String msg,
                                Throwable exception) {
        this(msg);
        this.exception = exception;
    } // constructor(String)
    /**
     * Returns the exception that gave rise to this or null.
     */
    public Throwable getException() {
        return exception;
    } // getException()

    /**
     * Print a stack trace of the exception.
     */
    public void printStackTrace() {
        printStackTrace(System.err);
    } // printStackTrace()

    /**
     * Prints a stack trace of the exception
     * @param out The PrintStream to write the stack trace to.
     */
    public void printStackTrace(PrintStream out) {
        synchronized (out) {
            if (exception != null) {
                out.print("ApplicationException: ");
                exception.printStackTrace(out);
            } else {
                super.printStackTrace(out);
            } // if
        } // synchronized
    } // printStackTrace(PrintStream)
    ...
} // class ApplicationException
```

FORCES

- Suppose that a method calls a method of another class. If the called method throws an exception, the calling method has a dependency on the exception class. If the calling method does not catch the exception, it forces its callers to have a dependency on the exception class. If the calling method, its callers, and the exception class are related to the same problem domain, then the dependencies created because the calling method does not catch the exception are not necessarily bad.

■ If the exception class is related to a different problem domain, then by not catching the exception the calling method makes its callers dependent on a class outside their problem domain. Therefore, if a method will be called by other methods that are part of the same problem domain, the method should catch exceptions thrown to it that are related to a different problem domain.

SOLUTION

If a method and its callers are all related to the same problem domain and an exception related to a different problem domain is thrown by one of the method's callees, then the method should catch the exception. If the method is not the appropriate place to handle the exception, it should handle the exception by throwing an exception related to the problem domain.

CONSEQUENCES

■ A method that catches rather than throws exceptions that do not relate to its problem domain avoids requiring its callers to have a dependency on an exception class that is part of an unrelated problem domain.

■ Methods that do not have to deal with exception classes unrelated to their problem domain are easier to understand, more cohesive, simpler, and easier to maintain.

IMPLEMENTATION

When implementing the Convert Exceptions pattern, substituting an application-domain-related exception for a domain-unrelated exception should not result in the loss of the information in the original exception. In particular, it is important to maintain the original stack trace. The `ApplicationException` class shown at the end of the "Context" section for this pattern shows how the original stack trace information can be retained by having the application-domain-related exception delegate `printStackTrack` to the replaced exception.

It is also important to allow the code that ultimately handles the exception to be able to dig deeper and get access to the original exception. The `getException` method shown in the listing of the `ApplicationException` class provides this access.

JAVA API USAGE

As of version 1.2 of Java, the `forName` method of the `Class` class fully implements the Convert Exceptions pattern. If a call to the `forName` method initiates the loading of a class and an exception is thrown during the class's initialization, the `forName` method throws a `ClassNotFoundException` in place of the original exception.

RELATED PATTERNS

Low Coupling/High Cohesion   The Low Coupling/High Cohesion pattern tells us to avoid unnecessary dependencies between classes.

Server Socket [Grand99]

SYNOPSIS

You need to write code to manage the server side of a socket-based network connection. The code that you write follows a very consistent pattern that revolves around `ServerSocket` and `Socket` objects.

CONTEXT

Programs that communicate with each other through socket-based connections play one of two roles in the establishment of a connection:

1. **Client.**   Programs in the client role initiate socket connections with a server.
2. **Server.**   Programs in the server role wait for clients to initiate connections with them.

   After a connection is established, programs in both the client and server roles interact with the connection in pretty much the same way.
   The basic logic that server programs use to manage the establishment of connections is consistent from one server program to the next because they all need to solve the same set of problems.

FORCES

- The constructor for the class `java.io.ServerSocket` performs the task of binding to a given port number and requesting that the operating system queue up connections on the program's behalf.

- You can use a `ServerSocket` object's `accept` method to accept client connections.
- A common requirement for server programs is that they be able to shut down in an orderly manner when they receive a command to do so. To accomplish this, a server program thread that is responsible for accepting connections must recognize the shutdown request, close the `ServerSocket` object, and perform any other appropriate cleanup actions.
- The default mode of operation for a `ServerSocket` object's `accept` method is to wait indefinitely for a client to initiate a connection. This can be inappropriate in some cases, because a thread cannot do other things, such as notice a shutdown request, while it is waiting for the `accept` method to return.
- You can set a time limit on how long the `ServerSocket` object's `accept` method will wait for a connection to accept by calling the `ServerSocket` object's `setSoTimeout` method.
- It is usually important that a server be able to process multiple connections concurrently. If a server can process only one connection at a time, clients may have to wait unreasonably long amounts of time to get a connection processed. The only exceptions to this are applications in which the server has so little to do that the delay for clients waiting to take their turn is not noticeable.
- To process multiple connections concurrently, a server will need more threads than the one that accepts connections.
- A common requirement for server programs is that it be possible to run more than one instance of the server program on the same host machine. This usually implies that each instance will use a different port number.
- `Socket` objects represent an established network connection. To communicate through an established connection, a program must get an `InputStream` or an `OutputStream` from the `Socket` object.
- When a server is finished with a connection, it should close the connection. This allows the local operating system to free up the resources it had committed to supporting the connection. The server also notifies the program at the other end of

the connection and its remote operating system to free up whatever resources they had committed to the connection.

SOLUTION

Most servers are implemented with code that follows a very consistent pattern.

1. Bind to a specific port. This means telling the operating system that if a client requests a connection to a server at that port, this program will accept the connection.
2. Ask the operating system to accept connections on behalf of the program when the program is not waiting to accept a connection. The operating system will then accept and queue up connections on behalf of the program, up to a maximum number of connections that is specified by the program.
3. Enter a loop that begins by accepting the next connection.
4. Check to see if the server has been requested to shut down.
5. Start processing the connection in a separate thread.
6. Get an `InputStream` and an `OutputStream` to communicate with the client over the connection.
7. Close the client when done.

The following listing of a simple server illustrates this pattern. The server's application-specific logic is that it reads a line of input from the client that should be the name of a file. If the server does not have a file with that name, it responds with a line of output that says

```
Bad file-name
```

If the server does have a file with that name, it responds with a line of output that says

```
Good
```

and follows it with the contents of the file.

Here is a listing of the server:

```
public class FileServer {
    // Default port number to listen on
    private final static int DEFAULT_PORT_NUMBER = 1234;

    // The maximum connections the operating system should
    // accept when the server is not waiting to accept one.
    private final static int MAX_BACKLOG = 20;

    // Timeout in milliseconds for accepting connections.
    // It may go this long before noticing a request to shut down.
    private final static int TIMEOUT = 500;

    // The port number to listen for connections on
    private int portNumber;

    // Set to true when server should shut down.
    private boolean shutDownFlag = false;

    private int activeConnectionCount = 0;
```

Two instances of the server cannot successfully listen on the same port to accept connections. To allow multiple instances of the server to run at the same time there are two constructors. One constructor takes no arguments and creates a server that listens for connection on DEFAULT_PORT_NUMBER. The other constructor takes one argument that specifies the port number on which the server will listen for connections.

```
public FileServer() {
    this(DEFAULT_PORT_NUMBER);
} // constructor()

public FileServer(int port) {
    portNumber = port;
} // constructor(int)

public int getActiveConnectionCount() {
    return activeConnectionCount;
} // getActiveConnectionCount()
```

This is the top-level method for the file server. It does not return until the server shuts down. It is common for this logic to be invoked by the Server class's constructor. The advantage in exposing this as a separate method is that it becomes possible to restart the server without having to create a new instance of it.

```
public void runServer() {
    ServerSocket s;

    try {
        // Create the ServerSocket.
        s = new ServerSocket(portNumber, MAX_BACKLOG);
```

The following listing sets a timeout for accepting connections so that the server won't wait for a long period of time to notice a request to shut down.

```
        s.setSoTimeout(TIMEOUT);
    } catch (IOException e) {
        System.err.println("Unable to create socket");
        e.printStackTrace();
        return;
    } // try
```

```
    // loop to keep accepting new connections
    try {
        Socket socket;
    serverLoop:
        while (true) { // Keep accepting connections.
            try {
                socket = s.accept(); // Accept a connection.
            } catch (java.io.InterruptedIOException e) {
                socket = null;
                if (!shutDownFlag)
                    continue serverLoop;
            } // try
```

The purpose of this `try` statement is to catch exceptions thrown by the call to `accept` because of the previously specified timeout. Timing out periodically gives the server an opportunity to check if it has been requested to shut down. Without the timeout, the server would not notice a shutdown request until it received its next connection. There is no limit on how long that could take. Having a half-second timeout ensures that it will take no longer than a half second for the server to notice a shutdown request; the following listing demonstrates this.

```
        if (shutDownFlag) {
            if (socket != null)
                socket.close();
            s.close();
            return;
```

```
            } // if
            // Create worker object to process connection.
            new FileServerWorker(s.accept());
        } // while
    } catch (IOException e) {
        // if there is an I/O error just return
    } // try
} // start()
/**
 * This is called to request the server to shut down.
 */
public void stop() {
    shutDownFlag = true;
} // shutDown()
```

The `FileServer` class contains a private inner class named
`FileServerWorker`. It creates an instance of this class to process
each connection.

```
private class FileServerWorker implements Runnable {
    private Socket s;

    FileServerWorker(Socket s) {
        this.s = s;
        new Thread(this).start();
    } // constructor(Socket)
```

A notable feature of the `FileServerWorker` class is that it
creates a new thread to process its connection.

```
public void run() {
    InputStream in;
    String fileName = "";
    PrintStream out = null;
    FileInputStream f;

    activeConnectionCount++;
    // get file name from client and open the file.
    try {
        in = s.getInputStream();
        out = new PrintStream(s.getOutputStream());
        fileName = new DataInputStream(in).readLine();
        f = new FileInputStream(fileName);
    } catch (IOException e) {
        activeConnectionCount--;
        if (out != null)
            out.print("Bad:"+fileName+"\n");
        out.close();
        try {
```

```
            s.close();
        } catch (IOException ie) {
        }
        return;
    } // try

    // send contents of file to client.
    out.print("Good:\n");
    byte[] buffer = new byte[4096];
    try {
        int len;
        while (!shutDownFlag && (len = f.read(buffer)) > 0)
{
            out.write(buffer, 0, len);
        } // while
    } catch (IOException e) {
    } finally {
        try {
            activeConnectionCount--;
            in.close();
            out.close();
            s.close();
        } catch (IOException e) {
        } // try
    } // try
} // run()
} // class FileServerWorker
} // class FileServer
```

CONSEQUENCES

Implementing servers with code similar to the listing under the "Solution" heading of this pattern provides them with certain capabilities:

- It's possible to run multiple instances of the server.
- You can configure each instance of the server to use a specified port number.
- The server is capable of processing multiple connections concurrently.
- Other classes can asynchronously request the server to shut down by calling the server's stop method.
- The server may not immediately notice a request to shut down. There is a maximum amount of time a server will take before it notices a request to shut down. The value of TIME-

OUT determines how long that is. In the listing, it is 500 milliseconds or 0.5 second.

■ The server closes the connection with its client when it is done.

IMPLEMENTATION

The code shown under the "Solution" heading for this pattern creates a new thread for every connection. This is not always the best method for implementing concurrency in a server. Some of the disadvantages of this technique are:

■ Threads can be particularly time-consuming to create.
■ Under some implementations of Java, threads can take a rather large amount of memory. In some cases, a thread can require more than 200K!
■ The pattern places no upper limit on the number of connections that are active at one time. This means that there is no limit on the number of threads the server has active. It can cause a server to become very slow because Java and the server's host machine spend an excessive amount of time managing the threads.

The Thread Pool pattern described in Volume 3 shows a better way for servers to manage threads.

RELATED PATTERNS

Client Socket   The Client Socket pattern describes the common logic for implementing clients.

Thread Pool   The Thread Pool pattern discussed in Volume 3 describes a more efficient way to manage server threads.

Two Phase Termination   The Two Phase Termination pattern found in Volume 1 explains how to use a `Thread` object's `interrupt` method to request that the thread shut down in an orderly manner.

Client Socket [Grand99]

SYNOPSIS

You need to write code to manage the server side of a socket-based network connection. The code that you write follows a very consistent pattern that revolves around `Socket` objects.

CONTEXT

Programs that communicate with each other through socket-based connections play one of two roles in the establishment of a connection:

1. **Client.** Programs in the client role initiate socket connections with a server.
2. **Server.** Programs in the server role wait for clients to initiate connections with them.

After a connection is established, programs in both the client and server roles interact with the connection in pretty much the same way.

The basic logic that client programs use to manage the establishment of connections is consistent from one client program to the next because they all need to solve the same set of problems.

FORCES

- Because client programs are responsible for initiating the creation of connections, client programs must be able to identify the server host with which they want to initiate a connection.

- The simplest way for a client to identify a server host is by its address, which is typically a sequence of numbers, such as 192.48.233.6.
- Client programs are usually required to identify a host by its name rather than its address. This is to give the people who administer the client's hosts some flexibility over which host will host the server program. If clients all identify a host by its name, then administrators can control which physical host the clients connect to by changing the definition of the name to be a different network address. They can do this without modifying or accessing the clients in any way.
- `Socket` objects represent an established network connection. To communicate with the program at the other end of a connection, a program must get an `InputStream` or an `OutputStream` from the `Socket` object.
- You can pass an address or a name to the constructor of a `Socket` object.
- When a client is finished with a connection, it should close the connection. This allows the local operating system to free up the resources it had committed to supporting the connection. It also notifies the program at the other end of the connection and its remote operating system to free up whatever resources they had committed to the connection.

SOLUTION

Most clients are implemented with code that follows a very consistent pattern.

1. Convert the name of the server's host machine to a network address.
2. Request a connection with the server.
3. Get an `InputStream` and an `OutputStream` to communicate with the server over the connection.
4. Perform the necessary task through the connection.
5. Close the connection when the task is complete.

The following listing of a simple client illustrates the pattern. The client's application-specific logic is that it writes a line of text to the server that is the name of a file. If the server does not have a file with that name, it responds with a line of output that says

Bad *file-name*

If the server has a file with that name, it responds with the line of output that says

Good

and follows it with the contents of the file.

Here is a listing of the client:

```java
public class FileClient {
    private static final int PORT = 1234;
    ...
    public static void main(String[] argv) {
        int exitCode = 0;

        if (!usageOk(argv))
          System.exit(1);
        Socket s = null;
        try {
            s = new Socket(argv[0], PORT);
        } catch (IOException e) {
            System.err.println("Unable to connect to server");
            e.printStackTrace();
            System.exit(1);
        } // try
        InputStream in = null;
        try {
            OutputStream out = s.getOutputStream();
            new PrintStream(out).print(argv[1]+"\n");
            int ch;
            in = new BufferedInputStream(s.getInputStream());
            DataInputStream din = new DataInputStream(in);
            String serverStatus = din.readLine();
            if (serverStatus.startsWith("Bad")) {
                exitCode = 1;
            } else {
                while((ch = in.read()) >= 0) {
                    System.out.write((char)ch);
                } // while
            } // if
        } catch (IOException e) {
```

```
        exitCode = 1;
    } finally {
        try {
            if (in != null)
                in.close();
            s.close();
        } catch (IOException e) {
        } // try
    } // try
    System.exit(exitCode);
} // main(String[])
} // class FileClient
```

CONSEQUENCES

- The client can connect to a server identified by a name or a network address.
- Once it establishes a connection with a server, the client can have a dialog with the server.
- The client closes the connection with the server when the task is complete.
- If the server goes down, the client has no way of directly detecting the problem. The Heartbeat pattern discussed in Volume 3 provides a way to deal with this problem.

RELATED PATTERNS

Heartbeat   The Heartbeat pattern described in Volume 3 provides a technique that allows a client program to detect that a server has gone down.

Server Socket   The Server Socket pattern describes the common logic that servers use to communicate with clients.

Coding Optimization
Patterns

The patterns in this chapter can be used to improve the performance of a program in ways that a compiler's automatic optimizations cannot accomplish. Like any other kind of optimization, you should use the patterns in this chapter only after you have established a definite need for them. For example, the Loop Unrolling pattern reduces the amount of time required to execute a loop. It does so at the expense of making the code larger and harder to understand and maintain. If the program makes enough loop iterations for a small reduction in the duration of each iteration to produce a noticeable improvement, it is appropriate to apply the Loop Unrolling pattern. If applying the Loop Unrolling pattern does not produce a noticeable improvement to your program, then you have made it more difficult to understand and maintain with no corresponding benefit.

The usual way to determine what to optimize is to run a program using a good execution-profiling tool. Such tools can tell you how much time a program spends in different methods or statements, the percentage of time that the program spent in each place, and the number of times that each statement or method was executed.

The places in which the program spends the most time are the appropriate places to optimize, because effort spent in those places will have the greatest payback.

Some patterns in this chapter arguably could be classified as design patterns rather than coding patterns. Although they do affect the organization of classes in a pattern, it may not be clear that they are appropriate until after you begin coding. For this reason, they are included in this chapter.

Hashed Adapter Objects [Grand99]

SYNOPSIS

Dispatch a method call to an adapter object associated with an arbitrary object. The arbitrary object is used to locate the adapter object in a hash table. The Hashed Adapter Objects pattern is most commonly used when an object must be created from unencapsulated data or when unencapsulated data must be dispatched to an object.

CONTEXT

Suppose a method is required to perform different actions based on a given object reference. A common technique for implementing this type of decision is to use a chain of if statements.

If the number of comparisons made using if statements is very large, then the amount of time it takes to perform the comparisons can be a performance issue. When an object reference must be compared with many other object references, there are faster techniques than using a chain of if statements.

This can be viewed as a searching problem. If you put the object references in a data structure, the problem is reduced to selecting a data structure that can be searched as quickly as possible. The data structure must also allow an additional object to be associated with each object reference. The purpose of the additional object is to determine what to do when an object reference within the data structure matches a given object reference.

The additional objects are adapter objects (see the Adapter pattern in Volume 1). In other words, they all implement a common interface. The interface defines a method that is called when the adapter object is fetched from the data structure. The adapter objects implement this method to call another object's method, which performs the desired action.

The data structure that best meets your needs is a *hash table*. On average, only about one comparison is required to locate an object in a hash table. The drawback to using a hash table is that when you fetch objects sequentially from it, the order of the objects is not predictable. Because that is not a problem here, a hash table seems optimal. The time required to locate an object in most other data structures varies with the number of objects in the data structure.

Let's consider a concrete example. Suppose that you are writing a program that has to both read and process a file. This file is organized into records. The design of the program requires the file to construct an object that encapsulates the contents of each record before using its contents. Figure 7.1 is a class diagram that shows part of this design.

A `FileProcessor` object reads groups of bytes from `FileInputStream` objects called *records*. Each record begins with a sequence of 8-bit characters that identify what type of record it is. The identifying sequence of characters is followed by a ":" character. What follows that ":" character varies with the type or record.

`FileInputStream` objects convert each record to a string. `FileProcessor` objects pass those strings to a `RecordFactory`

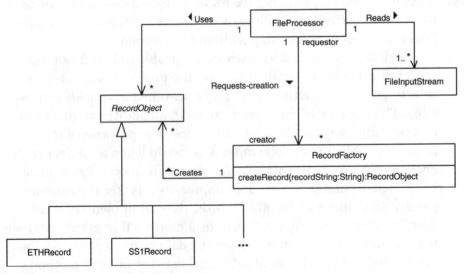

FIGURE 7.1 Encapsulate records in objects.

object's `createRecord` method. The `createRecord` method returns an instance of a concrete subclass of the `ReadObject` class. The record type determines the subclass of `ReadObject`.

When the time comes to tune your program, you find that it spends a disproportionate amount of time in the `RecordFactory` class's `createRecord` method. You notice that there are over 300 types of records. The test to determine the type of a record is coded as a chain of `if` statements like this:

```
if (type.equals("ETH"))
  return new ETHRecord(record);
else if (type.equals("SS1"))
  return new SS1Record(record);
...
```

You conclude that a lookup in a hash table will be a lot faster than those string comparisons. The cost of looking up a string in a hash table is typically equivalent to just a few string comparisons. To implement this idea, you add some classes to your design, as shown in the class diagram in Figure 7.2.

In the optimized implementation shown in Figure 7.2, a class has been added to the design that corresponds to each subclass of `RecordObject`. These classes implement an interface called `RecordCreatorIF`. Instances of these classes are responsible for creating instances of the corresponding `RecordObject` class. A `RecordFactory` object uses objects that implement the `RecordCreatorIF` interface to create instances of concrete subclasses of `RecordObject`.

During its initialization, a `RecordFactory` object creates one instance of each class that implements the `RecordCreatorIF` interface. It associates each of these objects with a string that contains the sequence of characters that identify the record type of the `RecordObject` subclass, which the `RecordCreatorIF` object can instantiate. It delegates the maintenance of these associations to a `HashMap` object.

A `RecordFactory` object passes each pair of string and `RecordCreatorIF` object to a `HashMap` object's `put` method so that each string is a key with the `RecordCreatorIF` object as its associated value.

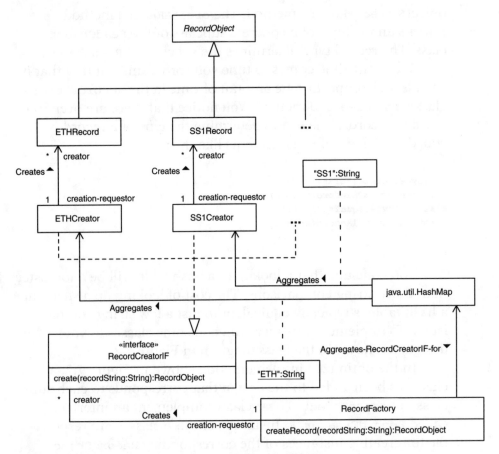

FIGURE 7.2 Hashed adapters to create RecordObjects.

As the program processes a file, it passes strings that contain the records it reads to a `RecordFactory` object's `createRecord` method. The `createRecord` method passes the substring that identifies the record type to the `HashMap` object's `get` method. The `get` method returns the `RecordCreatorIF` object associated with the substring. The `createRecord` method then makes a polymorphic call to the `RecordCreatorIF` object's `create` method, passing it the record string. This `create` method generates and returns an instance of its `RecordObject` class.

The collaboration diagram in Figure 7.3 shows an example of these interactions. It shows what happens when an SS1 record is passed to a `RecordFactory` object's `createRecord` method.

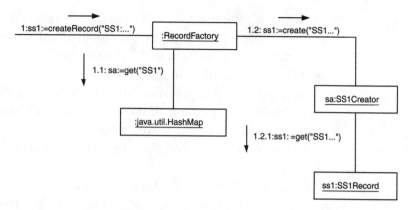

FIGURE 7.3 Creating an SS1Record object.

FORCES

- There is a long chain of `if` statements that performs `equals` tests between one object and many other objects; the chain of `if` statements takes a disproportionately large amount of execution time.
- An action performed is determined by `equals` comparisons between a single object and a variable set of other objects.
- The set of object-action pairs may grow, shrink, or otherwise vary over time.
- A hash table data structure allows a value associated with a key object to be found in an amount of time that is relatively independent of the number of objects in the hash table, provided that certain conditions are met. Hash table data structures are discussed in more detail under the "Implementation" heading for this pattern.
- If there are only a few objects to be tested, the hash table lookup may take longer than a chain of `if` statements. As with all optimizations, it's best to determine through actual timings whether the hash table lookup is faster than a chain of `if` statements. Even if the chain of `if` statements is long, if a few objects are chosen much more frequently than the others, it may be possible to achieve better results by placing those objects at the beginning of the `if` chain.

- Although the use of a hash table may result in faster execution, a hash table and adapter classes will consume more memory than a chain of `if` statements.
- The shear number of adapter classes created may take a prohibitively long amount of time to write. However, it's often the case that adapter classes have a strong structural similarity to each other. Sometimes they vary in as few ways as the name of the class and the name of the method that they call.

If they are structurally similar it is usually possible to automate most of their creation using such tools as editor macros or stand-alone macro processors.

SOLUTION

The assumptions related to the Hashed Adapter Objects pattern are a set of actions and a corresponding set of objects. When an action is selected and then performed, a program makes comparisons between a given object and the objects in the set that uses their `equals` method. If one of the objects in the set is equal to the given object, the action that corresponds to that object is performed. The class diagram found in Figure 7.4 shows the organization that the Hashed Adapter Objects pattern provides for handling this.

Following are descriptions for the roles that objects, classes, and interfaces play in the Hashed Adapter Objects pattern:

ActionIF   An interface in this role defines a method, shown in the diagram in Figure 7.4 as `doIt`, that a `Client` class can call to get an action performed.

Action1, Action2   Classes in these roles implement an `ActionIF` interface and encapsulate a behavior used by a client object. Many of these classes do not directly implement the behavior, but are adapter classes that delegate the behavior to another class that does not implement the `ActionIF` interface.

ActionKey1, ActionKey2   Objects in this role have an instance of one of the Action1, Action2, . . . classes associated with them.

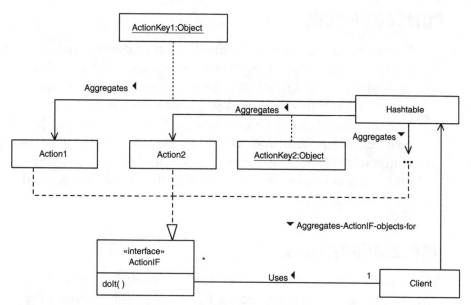

FIGURE 7.4 Hashed adapters classes.

Hashtable   Instances of classes in this role are responsible for associating an instance of one of the Action1, Action2, . . . classes with objects in the ActionKey1, ActionKey2, . . . role. When a `Client` object presents an instance of a `Hashtable` with an ActionKey1, ActionKey2, . . . object, it finds a corresponding ActionKey1, ActionKey2, . . . object already stored in the hash table. To be a corresponding object, the given object's `equals` method must return true when the `Hashtable` object passes it one of the ActionKey1, ActionKey2, . . . objects already stored in the hash table. After it finds the corresponding object, it returns the instance of one of the Action1, Action2, . . . classes associated with the corresponding object.

Client   When an instance of a class in this role needs to perform an action associated with an object, it presents that object to a `Hashtable` object. The `Hashtable` object returns to it an object that implements an `ActionIF` interface. The `Client` object then calls that object's `doIt` method to perform the required action.

CONSEQUENCES

■ If a Hashtable class is well tuned, most of the cost for retrieving an action object from a Hashtable object will be one call to the given object's hashCode method and an average of one call to an ActionKey object's equals method.

■ The set of ActionKey objects in a Hashtable object can be changed during runtime, as well as the Action objects associated with them. This means the set of objects associated with actions can be varied, as well as the actions associated with those objects.

IMPLEMENTATION

A hash table data structure associates key objects with value objects. This allows the associated value object for an object that is in the hash table as a key object to be found quickly.

The way that a hash table data structure works is when it is given a key object to store or find, it calls that object's hashCode method. It uses the value returned by the hashCode method to determine where in the data structure the object will be stored or looked for. The hashCode method returns an int value, so there will generally be more possible hash code values than there will be places in the data structure. Hash table algorithms resolve this difficulty by associating each place in the data structure with multiple hash code values. This means that multiple objects may want to be stored in the same place in a hash table. When this actually happens it is called a *collision*.

When there are no collisions, getting the value object associated with a key object involves the following steps:

1. Call the key object's hashCode method.
2. Look at the place in the data structure where the hash code says that the key object should be located if it exists in the data structure.
3. Determine if the key object is in the data structure.
4. If the key object exists in the data structure, return the associated value object.

Different hash table algorithms handle collisions differently. However, all techniques for handling collisions require additional searching when looking for an object at a place in the data structure in which there is a collision. Therefore, the time it takes to find something in a hash table is independent of the number of things in the hash table if no collisions exist.

It is not generally possible to prevent collisions in a hash table. However, you can arrange for collisions to be unlikely. Usually, the most important thing to control is how full you allow a hash table to become. If a hash table contains more objects than it has places to store them, it is certain that the hash table contains collisions. As a hash table goes from being 100 percent full to empty, the likelihood that the hash table contains collisions drops from 100 percent to 0 percent. Classes that implement a hash table data structure usually provide a way of specifying an upper limit on how full a hash table may become. If the hash table exceeds the limit, the hash table is enlarged to keep it within the limit.

The performance of hash tables is also affected by the quality of the `hashCode` methods implemented by the objects stored in the hash table. If the `hashCode` method of two different objects returns the same value, storing them both in a hash table will always produce a collision. Therefore, it is important that `hashCode` methods are implemented in a way that makes it unlikely that the `hashCode` method of two unequal objects will return the same value.

Java's core API provides two implementations of a hash table data structure: `java.util.Hashtable` and `java.util.hashMap`. You will usually use one of these two classes when implementing the Hashed Adapter Objects pattern. From an optimization perspective, the main difference between the two classes is that the methods for accessing data in the `java.util.Hashtable` class are synchronized and the methods in the `java.util.hashMap` class are not synchronized.

For applications of the Hashed Adapter Objects pattern in which the contents of the hash table data structure are initialized and then never changed, the `java.util.HashMap` class is a better choice, because many implementations of Java will take less time to call the unsynchronized methods of the `java.util.HashMap` class than the synchronized methods of the `java.util.Hashtable` class.

For applications of the Hashed Adapter Objects pattern in which the contents of the hash table data structure may be accessed by multiple threads, the `java.util.Hashtable` class is often the better choice. You will need to ensure that only one thread at a time accesses the hash table data structure. Usually the simplest way to do this is to take advantage of the fact that the methods of the `java.util.Hashtable` class are all synchronized.

JAVA API USAGE

The `java.awt.swing.JComponent` class uses the Hashed Adapter Objects pattern to manage key bindings. You can pass combinations of `KeyStroke` objects and `ActionListener` objects to a `JComponent` object's `registerKeyboardAction` method. The `registerKeyboardAction` method puts the combination in a `Hashtable` object.

When a `JComponent` object receives a `KeyEvent`, it gets the `KeyStroke` object associated with the `KeyEvent`. It then asks its `Hashtable` object for the `ActionListener` object associated with the `KeyStroke` object. If the `Hashtable` object returns such an `ActionListener` object, the `JComponent` object calls its `actionPerformed` method so that the action associated with the keystroke is performed.

CODE EXAMPLE

Following are listings of selected portions of the code that implements the design discussed under the Context heading of this pattern. The first is a skeletal listing of a sample subclass of `RecordObject`. This listing shows that the `SS1Record` class, like the other subclasses of `RecordObject`, has a constructor that takes a record string as an argument.

```
class SS1Record extends RecordObject {
    ...
    SS1Record(String recordString) {
        ...
    } // constructor(String)
    ...
} // class SS1Record
```

The adapter classes that are used to create instances of SS1Record and other subclasses of RecordObject all implement the RecordCreatorIF interface, which follows:

```
interface RecordCreatorIF {
    public RecordObject create(String recordString);
} // interface RecordCreatorIF
```

Following is a listing of an adapter class that implements the RecordCreatorIF interface's create method to invoke the constructor of the corresponding subclass of RecordObject:

```
class SS1Creator implements RecordCreatorIF {
    public RecordObject create(String recordString) {
        return new SS1Record(recordString);
    } // create
} // class SS1Creator
```

Finally, the following is a listing of the RecordFactory class that is responsible for managing the creation of RecordObject objects:

```
class RecordFactory {
    private HashMap creators;

RecordFactory() {
        creators = new HashMap(700, .5f);
        creators.put("ETH", new ETHCreator());
        creators.put("SS1", new SS1Creator());
        ...
    } // constructor()

    /**
     * Create and return an instance of the concrete subclass of
     * RecordObject that corresponds to the given record type in
     * the given record string.
     * @exception IllegalArgumentException if the object cannot be
     *            created because the contents of the record string
     *            are not valid.
     */
```

```
RecordObject createRecord(String recordString)
            throws IllegalArgumentException{
    //get record type
    int i = recordString.indexOf(':');
    if (i < 1) {
        throw new IllegalArgumentException(recordString);
    } // if
    String recordType = recordString.substring(0, i);
    // Create the recordObject
    RecordCreatorIF creator;
    creator = (RecordCreatorIF)creators.get(recordType);
    if (creator == null) {
        throw new IllegalArgumentException(recordType);
    } // if
    return creator.create(recordString);
} // createRecord(String)
} // class RecordFactory
```

RELATED PATTERNS

Adapter   The Hashed Adapter Objects pattern uses Adapter objects. The Adapter pattern is described in Volume 1.

Lookup Table   Both the Hashed Adapter Objects pattern and the Lookup Table pattern involve the use of an aggregation. However, the aggregation serves a different purpose for each. The Lookup Table pattern uses an aggregation of precomputed results to save the time it would take to compute those results in the future. For the Hashed Adapter Objects pattern, it is that data structure that implements the aggregation that is the source of the time savings.

Polymorphism   When it's possible to select a behavior based on the type of an object, the Polymorphism pattern produces a simpler result than the Hashed Adapter Objects pattern.

Single Threaded Execution   The Single Threaded Execution pattern is used to coordinate access by multiple threads to the hash table used by the Hashed Adapter Objects pattern. The Single Threaded Execution pattern is described in Volume 1.

Strategy   The Hashed Adapter Objects pattern can be used to design the selection of strategy objects in the Strategy pattern, which is described in Volume 1.

Lazy Initialization [Beck97]

SYNOPSIS

Delay the creation of an object or other expensive action needed to initialize a variable until it is known that the variable will be used.

CONTEXT

Suppose that you are responsible for maintaining the portion of a word processor program that wraps the words of a paragraph into lines. To avoid repeating the expense of determining where words begin and end, you have organized paragraph objects so that they contain characters and words that contain characters. The class diagram found in Figure 7.5 shows this organization.

The organization includes a common interface that both the DocWord and DocCharacter classes implement. This interface

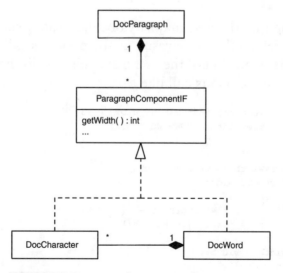

FIGURE 7.5 Paragraph organization.

specifies a method called getWidth. The getWidth method returns the width of the word or character with which it is associated.

This organization makes it very simple for a DocParagraph object to organize the objects that constitute it into lines. As it adds objects to a line, it calls their getWidth method. If there is still enough room on the line for the object, it adds the object to the line; otherwise, it starts a new line.

Suppose there have been complaints about the speed of refreshing the display as someone types into the middle of a paragraph. You have identified the problem area as the amount of time it takes for a paragraph to rewrap the objects it contains. Further analysis with a profiler shows this problem to be the amount of time that it spends getting the width of characters.

You notice that most of the calls to the DocCharacter class's getWidth method are made from the DocWord class's method from code that looks like this:

```
public int getWidth() {
    int width = 0;
    for (int i=0; i < length; i++) {
        width += chars[i].getWidth();
    } // for
    return width;
} // getWidth()
```

Realizing that the vast majority of calls to an object's getWidth method return the same result as the previous call, you modify the implementation of the getWidth method so that it retains the result of the previous call like this:

```
private static final int UNKNOWN_WIDTH = -1;
private int prevWidth = UNKNOWN_WIDTH;

public int getWidth() {
    if (prevWidth != UNKNOWN_WIDTH)
      return prevWidth;
    int width = 0;
    for (int i=0; i < length; i++) {
        width += chars[i].getWidth();
    } // for
    prevWidth = width;
    return width;
} // getWidth()
```

The new implementation strategy is to save the display width of a DocWord object in a variable, called prevWidth. The initial value of prevWidth is the distinguished value UNKNOWN_WIDTH. If the value of the prevWidth variable is UNKNOWN_WIDTH, it does not contain the DocWord object's display width. If this is the case when a DocWord object's getWidth method is called, it computes the object's display width and saves it in the prevWidth variable.

When anything happens to a DocWord object that changes its display width, it sets the value of its prevWidth variable back to UNKNOWN_WIDTH.

FORCES

- A variable is expensive to initialize and its value is not always used.
- Instances of a class perform a computation that always produces the same result.
- You must ensure that a variable is initialized before its value is fetched.

SOLUTION

The Lazy Initialization pattern consists of the following code elements:

- An instance or static variable. For reasons explained by the Maximize Privacy pattern, the variable is usually private.
- A distinguished value that can be assigned to the variable to indicate that it does not have a meaningful value. If the variable is declared to contain an object reference, then the distinguished value is usually null.
- An accessor method that is used to fetch the value of the variable when the accessor method is called. If the value of the variable is the distinguished value, the method is responsible for computing a valid value for the variable and setting the variable to that value. All code, even in the same class,

should use the accessor method to retrieve the variable's value. If all fetches of the variable's value are through the accessor method, it is easy to ensure that the variable is initialized before its value is first fetched.

- Any code that recognizes an event that implies a different value for the variable must set the value of the variable to be the distinguished value.

The following code contains those elements:

```
class LazyInitialization {
    ...
    private Foo foo = null;

    Foo getFoo() {
        if (foo == null)
            foo = computeFoo();
        return foo;
    } // getFoo()

    void doIt() {

        getFoo().bar();

        ...

        if (...)

            foo = null;

        ...

    } // doIt()
} // class LazyInitialization
```

In this code, the Lazy Initialization pattern is applied to the variable foo. The distinguished value that indicates that foo does not have a valid value is null. The method that other pieces of code should use to fetch the variable's value is the getFoo method.

The doIt method is an example of code in the same class as the variable that accesses the variable through its accessor method. It is also an example of a method that detects that the current value of the variable is invalid, and sets the value of the variable to its distinguished value.

CONSEQUENCES

- The computation needed to set the variable to its proper value is never done if the value is never used. This saves time if there are situations in which the value is not needed.
- Applying the Lazy Initialization pattern to multiple variables in a program that would otherwise be initialized at about the same time spreads their initialization out over time. This can improve the perceived responsiveness of a program.
- Saving the result of a computation in a variable can save time by not having to repeat the computation.
- The Lazy Initialization pattern adds complexity to a class that would not be present if a variable is initialized by an initializer or constructor in the usual way.

JAVA API USAGE

The `java.util.Calendar` class allows the time and date represented by one of its instances to be specified as either a discrete value, such as year, month, day, and so forth, or as a single `long` value. It does not automatically convert between the two different representations. Instead, it only performs a conversion when the date or time is requested in a form different from what was provided.

RELATED PATTERNS

Maximize Privacy　The Maximize Privacy pattern provides a justification for making a lazily initialized variable private.

Virtual Proxy　Like the Lazy Initialization pattern, the Virtual Proxy pattern can be used to delay a computation or the creation of an object until it is actually needed. The difference is that the Virtual Proxy pattern uses a proxy object to hide the computation; the Lazy Initialization pattern uses a method to hide the computation.

Double-Checked Locking [Schmidt-Harrison96]

SYNOPSIS

A multithreaded program does not initialize a resource until it actually requires the resource. One thread recognizes that the resource is not yet initialized when another thread has already begun the initialization. Avoid duplicating the initialization effort by coordinating the actions of multiple threads.

CONTEXT

Suppose you have some code that is responsible for creating an object if it does not already exist. The code can look something like this:

```
private CabinetAssistantIF assistant = null;
...
CabinetAssistantIF getCabinetAssistant() {
    if (assistant == null) {
    ...
    } // if
    return assistant;
} // getCabinetAssistant()
```

If it is possible for the getCabinetAssistant method to be called by more than one thread at a time, then there may be problems with this code. At the very least, multiple threads can create an assistant object, though only one needs to do so. It can also be that if the object is created more than once, then the program may not behave correctly. For these reasons and to avoid wasted effort, it will be important to ensure that the object is created only once.

One way to avoid multiple threads creating the assistant object is to declare the getCabinetAssistant method to be synchronized. This solves the problem of multiple threads creating the assistant object. However, it introduces a new performance concern.

Declaring the getCabinetAssistant method to be synchronized means that threads will be forced to obtain a synchronization lock before they even determine if the assistant object has already been created. Threads could be forced to wait for other threads to simply check if the assistant object has already been created. Even if a thread does not have to wait for a synchronization lock, getting and releasing a synchronization lock takes longer than just checking to see if the assistant object has already been created.

There is a way of coding this so that the assistant object is only created once, and after it is created there is no additional time spent waiting for or obtaining a synchronization lock. Consider the following revised code:

```
private CabinetAssistantIF assistant = null;
...
CabinetAssistantIF getCabinetAssistant() {
    if (assistant == null) {
        synchronized (this) {
            if (assistant == null) {
                ...
            } // if
        } // synchronized
    } // if
    return assistant;
} // getCabinetAssistant()
```

In this version, the getCabinetAssistant method checks to see if the assistant object has already been created. If it has not been created, the getCabinetAssistant method gets a synchronization lock and then checks a second time to see if the assistant object has already been created. The synchronized statement and the if statement that follows it ensure that only one assistant object can be created. The second if statement ensures that if two threads make it past the first if statement, only the first thread to get a synchronization lock does the initialization. After the assistant object is created, the first if statement prevents the synchronized statement from being executed, thus avoiding the unnecessary delays and additional overhead that the synchronized statement would cause.

FORCES

- An initialization should only be performed once.
- There are multiple threads that can perform an initialization.
- The test to determine if the initialization has been completed is very inexpensive.

SOLUTION

To ensure an initialization will only be performed once when there are multiple threads that can potentially perform the initialization, check twice to see if the initialization has already been performed: Check once before getting a synchronization lock and once after. The code for this has the following general form:

```
if (isInitialized()) {
    synchronized (this) {
        if (isInitialized()) {
            ...
        } // if
    } // synchronized
} // if
```

CONSEQUENCES

- The initialization is performed only once, even if multiple threads attempt to perform the initialization at the same time.
- The additional overhead introduced by the Double-Checked Locking pattern is low, because the initialization is performed only once and the cost of determining if the initialization has been performed is low.
- The reason for having two if statements may not be obvious to someone reading the code without a comment explaining it.

RELATED PATTERNS

Balking   The Balking design pattern described in Volume 1 is usually implemented using the same if-synchronized-if structure as the Double-Checked Locking pattern.

Lazy Initialization   The Double-Checked Locking pattern can be used to ensure the integrity of the Lazy Initialization pattern when it is used in multithreaded application.

Singleton   The Double-Checked Locking pattern can be used in a thread-safe and efficient implementation of the Singleton pattern described in Volume 1.

Virtual Proxy   The Double-Checked Locking pattern can be used in a thread-safe implementation of the Virtual Proxy pattern described in Volume 1.

Loop Unrolling [Grand99]

This pattern is based on techniques described in the book, *Compilers, Principles, Techniques and Tools,* by Alfred V. Aho, Ravi Seti, and Jeffery D. Ullman [Aho-et al.86].

SYNOPSIS

Reduce the overhead of a loop's control logic by increasing the amount of work it performs in each iteration, so it can accomplish the same amount of work in fewer iterations. This pattern trades memory for speed.

CONTEXT

Suppose you have to speed up the following loop:

```
void solarize(int[] pixels) {
    for (int i=0; i<pixels.length; i++) {
        pixels[i] ^= 0x00ffffff;
    } // for
} // solarize(int[])
```

Profiling indicates that the loop spends more than half of its time in its control logic—testing the value of i, incrementing i, and branching back. On a typical call, the loop will iterate over 4000 times. You know you can speed up the loop by increasing the amount of work it does in each iteration so that fewer iterations are required. With this idea in mind, you modify the code to the following:

```
void solarize(int[] pixels) {
    int i = pixels.length-1;
    for (; i>=99; i-=100) {
        pixels[i] ^= 0x00ffffff;
        pixels[i-1] ^= 0x00ffffff;
        ...
```

```
        pixels[i-98] ^= 0x00ffffff;
        pixels[i-99] ^= 0x00ffffff;
    } // for
    for (; i>=0; i--) {
        pixels[i] ^= 0x00ffffff;
    } // for
} // solarize(int[])
```

Your new code is restructured into two loops. The first handles 100 array elements per iteration. The second loop handles the remaining array elements, one per iteration. The new code runs in about half the time that it took the original code.

A good optimizing compiler may automatically unroll loops if it knows that they will iterate enough times to make the optimization worthwhile. In the preceding example, it is not possible for a compiler to make that determination.

FORCES

- A substantial portion of the time spent in a loop is spent in its control logic.
- The loop iterates enough times that reducing the amount of time spent in its control logic will improve a program's execution time.
- A compiler may be smart enough to automatically unroll some loops. It is not reasonable for compilers to automatically unroll many loops, because they do not have enough information about how many times the loop will be executed.

SOLUTION

Reorganize a loop that iterates many times to manipulate a small amount of information with each iteration into two loops. The first of the loops iterates fewer times but typically manipulates one to two orders of magnitude more information per iteration. The second loop is structured so that each of its iterations manipulate exactly as much information as the original loop. The purpose of the second loop is to process the relatively small amount of information that is left over after the first loop finishes.

The following is a somewhat more abstract example of this than appears under the Context heading for this pattern. Here is a loop in its basic form:

```
void foo(int count) {
    for (; count>0; count--) {
        doIt(count);
    } // for
} // foo(int)
```

If the loop iterates enough times so that its control logic is worth tuning, the loop can be unrolled into these two loops:

```
void foo(int count) {
    for (; count>100; count-=100) {
        doIt(count);
        doIt(count-1);
        doIt(count-2);
        ...
        doIt(count-98);
        doIt(count-99);
    } // for

    for (; count>0; count--) {
        doIt(count);
    } // for
} // foo(int)
```

The first loop handles 100 values of count per iteration; the second loop handles any leftover values.

There is an additional refinement, called *Duff's Device*, that can often be applied to loops that only iterate a moderate number of times. It takes advantage of two characteristics of switch statements.

1. Unless the code for a case contains a control flow–altering statement such as break or return, when that case is executed control flows into the next case.
2. Compilers usually generate code for a switch statement, which allows control to flow from the beginning of a switch statement to the proper case using a small and fixed number of instructions.

Using these observations, the second of the two loops can be reorganized to a switch `statement` so that its control logic uses a small and fixed number of instructions. The following listing demonstrates this.

```
switch (count) {
  case 99:
    doIt(99);
  case 98:
    doIt(98);
  ...
  case 2:
    doIt(2);
  case 1:
    doIt(1);
} // switch
```

This `switch` statement directs the flow of control to the case that corresponds to the values of count that are to be processed. Control flows from that case to the bottom of the `switch` statement.

Duff's Device was originally described by Tom Duff in a Usenet posting, which is reproduced at *www.mindspring.com/~mgrand/duffs-device.html* [Duff88].

CONSEQUENCES

- After being unrolled, fewer instructions are executed to perform the loop, but its code is larger and takes up more memory.
- In some cases, the fewer instruction executions may not take less time. For example, suppose the Java implementation executes programs as native machine instructions. Many computers have fast cache memory associated with their CPU. If a loop fits entirely within a cache, it executes more quickly. If the original loop fits in a cache but the unrolled version does not, the unrolled version may take longer to execute.
- Some Java implementations may automatically optimize some loops in ways that are better than explicit loop unrolling. You should always test the results of this opti-

mization on the intended Java implementation to ensure that it improves performance.

- You should test the effects of unrolling a loop in the environment(s) in which your program will execute, to determine its actual effect.
- Unrolling loops in source code can add greatly to the effort required to maintain the loop. Changes to the loop body require a lot more editing.

Lookup Table [Grand99]

SYNOPSIS

Save the memory consumed by complex code and the time it takes to execute by precomputing the results and putting them in a lookup table.

CONTEXT

Suppose you have to design a program that will find scheduled commercial airline flights between any two airports. One approach is to design the program to find all the combinations of flights that directly or indirectly go from one given airport to the other. There will be some constraints on the search, such as connecting flights may not be more than 23 hours apart and a combination of flights must not visit the same airport more than once. Even with those constraints, the program may have to consider hundreds of thousands of combinations of flights to find all combinations.

To avoid the program having to spend a great deal of time searching for flight routes, you store all the combinations of flights between each pair of airports that satisfy the constraints in a database.

FORCES

- Classification methods can involve long sequences of bulky conditional logic.
- Searches on some data can take a long time. For example, finding the shortest route between two cities on a road map can take an exponentially long amount of time because the search for the shortest route may have to consider an enormous number of combinations of roads.

- Some mathematical formulas take a long time to compute.
- If a computation always produces the same result for a given input, it is possible to represent the computation as a table that allows the result of the computation to be looked up by its input values.
- Storing precomputed results in a table may take an unacceptably large amount of memory if the results are large, there are a large number of results, or there is only a small amount of memory available.

SOLUTION

Suppose you have a computation that always produces the same results for the same inputs and the number of different combinations of inputs that are possible is reasonable. Consider precomputing the result of the computation for each combination of input values and storing the results in a table for later retrieval.

CONSEQUENCES

- If the table lookup is faster for doing the computation, your program will run faster.
- Some forms of lookup tables take up less memory than the code for the computation.

IMPLEMENTATION

It is common, when using the Lookup Table pattern, to represent the table as a single array. In many cases there is more than one piece of information that needs to be kept in lookup tables. If you represent a lookup table as an array, it is always possible to represent multiple pieces of information in that lookup table as multiple arrays.

A common technique for avoiding the need for multiple arrays is to encode multiple pieces of information into each array element. There are many ways to do this. So long as decoding the contents of an array element does not take longer than getting the pieces of information out of multiple arrays, it is a good design trade-off.

The example mentioned under both the "Java API Usage" heading and the "Code Example" heading for this pattern represents multiple pieces of information in array elements.

JAVA API USAGE

The `java.lang.Character` class uses the Lookup Table pattern. It contains arrays that allow it to classify Unicode characters. The array lookups are faster than executing an equivalent chain of `if` statements, and the arrays also take up less memory than the equivalent chain of `if` statements.

Part of what makes the arrays compact is that they use different bits of `int` values to indicate different attributes of characters, rather than use an array for each attribute.

CODE EXAMPLE

The calculation of the date on which a holiday falls in a particular year can be a bit complex for some holidays. The following code can be used to determine the date of Easter for any year in the range 1583 to 4099 using the Gregorian calendar.

```
private static final int MIN_EASTER_YEAR = 1583;
private static final int MAX_EASTER_YEAR = 4099;
...
public static GregorianCalendar easter(int year) {
    if (year < MIN_EASTER_YEAR || year > MAX_EASTER_YEAR) {
        throw new IllegalArgumentException(Integer.toString(year));
    } // if

    int a,b,c,h,l,m;
    a=year%19;
    b=year/100;
    c=year%100;
    h=(19*a+b-(b/4)-((b-((b+8)/25)+1)/3)+15)%30;
    l=(32+2*(b%4)+2*(c/4)-h-(c%4))%7;
    m=(a+11*h+22*l)/451;
    return new GregorianCalendar(year,
```

```
        (h+1-7*m+114)/31,
        (h+1-7*m+114)%31 + 1);
} // easter(int)
```

Suppose this code is incorporated into a calendar server that will be called upon to compute all the holidays in a month or year for multiple users at the same time. The holiday calculation for concurrent users is a performance problem, so you want to speed up the calculation Easter. You decide that you can speed it up by using the Lookup Table pattern.

You want to keep the date on which Easter falls in every year from 1583 to 4099 in an array. You would like to keep the representation compact, but not take much time to decode. What you decide is that rather than use two arrays to contain the month and date of each year's Easter, you use a single array of bytes to represent both the month and date of each year's Easter.

Each byte of the array corresponds to a year. The value in each byte is the day of the month (1–31) times 5 plus the month (3 or 4). The version of the code that uses a table to find the date of Easter in a year is as follows:

```
private static final int MIN_EASTER_YEAR = 1583;
private static final int MAX_EASTER_YEAR = 4099;
    ...
private static final int MONTH_MULTIPLIER = 32;

/**
 * The month and day of easter is encoded in this array.
 * A given year is represented in the array element at
 * index of year-1583.
 * The value in each element is month*32+day.
 */
private static byte[] easterDates = {
        (byte)138, (byte)129, (byte)149, (byte)134, (byte)125,
        (byte)145, (byte)130, (byte)150, (byte)142, (byte)125,
        (byte)146, (byte)138, (byte)122, (byte)142, (byte)134,
    ...
        (byte)153, (byte)138, (byte)130, (byte)150, (byte)134,
        (byte)125, (byte)146, (byte)131, (byte)121, (byte)142,
        (byte)134, (byte)147
    };
```

```
/**
 * Return a calendar object that contains the date of Easter on the
 * Gregorian calendar for the given year.
 * @param year the given year
 * @exception IllegalArgumentException if year is less than 1583
 *                                     or greater than 4099
 */
public static GregorianCalendar easter(int year) {
    if (year < MIN_EASTER_YEAR || year > MAX_EASTER_YEAR) {
        throw new IllegalArgumentException(Integer.toString(year));
    } // if

    // Because byte is a signed type, we must mask out the
    // higher order bits.
    int encoding = easterDates[year-MIN_EASTER_YEAR] & 0xff;
    return new GregorianCalendar(year,
                                 encoding/MONTH_MULTIPLIER,
                                 encoding%MONTH_MULTIPLIER);
} // easter(int)
```

RELATED PATTERNS

Hashed Adapter   Both the Hashed Adapter Objects pattern and
the Lookup Table pattern involve the use of an aggregation.
However, the aggregation serves a different purpose for each.
The Lookup Table pattern uses an aggregation of precomputed
results to save the time it would take to compute those results
in the future. For the Hashed Adapter Objects pattern, it's that
data structure that implements the aggregation, which is the
source of the time savings.

C H A P T E R

8

Code Robustness
Patterns

The patterns in this chapter describe ways to make code more robust. Most of them also have the effect of adding overhead of some sort.

Assertion Testing [Grand99]

SYNOPSIS

Verify that a method conforms to its contract with its callers by inserting code to test its preconditions, postconditions, invariants, and data conditions at runtime.

CONTEXT

A good technique for designing a method is to determine the conditions it must satisfy. There are different types of conditions that a method may need to satisfy. The most common are:

Preconditions.   Preconditions are conditions that must be true when a method is invoked. Such conditions often govern the arguments passed to the method, the state of the object the method is associated with, or a resource that the method manipulates. Typical preconditions are that an argument must be greater than zero, that an instance variable must not be null, or that a file must be open.

Postconditions.   Postconditions are conditions that must be true when a method returns. Such conditions often govern the method's return value, the state of the method associated with an object, or a resource that the method manipulates. Typical postconditions are that a return value has a particular relationship to the method's arguments, that an instance variable is initialized in a particular way, or that a file is closed.

Invariants.   Invariants are conditions that must be true during the entire duration of a method call. Such conditions often govern the state of the object that the method is associated with or a resource that the method manipulates. Typical invariants are that one instance variable must remain greater in value than another or that a queue cannot exceed a certain size.

Data Conditions. Data conditions are conditions that must be true at a particular point in a method's execution. A method's data conditions often govern the value that is returned by other methods that it calls.

Including conditions such as these when writing a specification for a method results in a specification that is very precise. Such specifications are easier to implement correctly than less precise specifications.

This technique of including conditions in a method's specification that essentially constitute a contract between a method and its callers is sometimes called *design by contract.* Design by contract is described in greater detail in Bertrand Meyer's article, *Applying Design by Contract* [Meyer92].

When you need to debug a program, it is important to be aware of the conditions that its methods must satisfy when they behave correctly. Bugs are often found by detecting differences between a method's contract and its observed behavior. Comments that explicitly document a method's contract make it easier for someone not familiar with the code to track down bugs.

Comments that specify a method's contract can reduce the amount of time spent on manual debugging. Automatic detection of a contract violation reduces debugging time even further.

FORCES

- You can specify much of a method's expected behavior as conditions that must be satisfied during the course of its execution.
- Tracking down bugs usually involves finding discrepancies between a method's contract with its callers and its actual behavior.
- In Java, it is customary to report abnormal or unexpected situations at runtime by throwing an exception. This applies

when an unsatisfied condition of a method's contract is detected. For reasons explained in the Checked versus Unchecked Exceptions pattern, exceptions thrown to report a contract violation should be unchecked exceptions.

- A method's caller is responsible for satisfying a method's preconditions.
- If a method's preconditions are to be enforced, the method must either take responsibility for enforcing its own preconditions or delegate that enforcement to another method that it calls.
- If a method's postconditions or invariant conditions are not satisfied, this indicates a programming error in the method. Programming errors are not part of a method's contract with its callers.
- A compiler that is able to parse and understand assertions that appear in specially formatted comments may be able to evaluate some assertions at compile time. There are advantages to having a compiler that is able to tell at compile time whether an assertion will be true or false at runtime. It means early detection of violated conditions. It also means that the compiler will not need to generate code for assertions that it determines are always true at compile time.

    If the compiler is not able to determine whether an assertion will be true or false at runtime, it will have to generate code to test the assertion at runtime. A disadvantage of runtime assertion testing is that condition violations are not detected until the corresponding assertions are executed in a circumstance that violates the condition. If testing is not done very carefully, a condition violation may occur after the program has been put into production.

- At the time of this writing, the author is not aware of any Java compilers that evaluate assertions at compile time. However, there are preprocessors that preprocess assertions embedded in specially formatted comments into live assertion-testing code.
- You may not want code to test assertions at runtime to be included in the version of a program that you put into pro-

duction. A good reason to omit assertion-testing code from production is that the program has been so well tested that the code provides no benefit to offset the addition memory and execution time it consumes. On the other hand, if a system is expected to evolve over time, the added protection of runtime assertion testing may be sufficiently valuable that it offsets the performance penalty.

SOLUTION

Include code in a method's source code that asserts the conditions that constitute the method's contract.

If you have access to a preprocessor that can preprocess assertions in specially formatted comments into assertion-testing code, then do supply the method's conditions as assertions in comments. An advantage that using a preprocessor has over creating assertion-testing code manually is that it is easier to manage postconditions. If a method has multiple exit points and you put assertion-testing code into the method manually, you will have to put tests for postconditions at each exit point. A preprocessor should be able to take a postcondition that you have stated once in a comment and automatically place it at all exit points.

If you do not have access to a suitable preprocessor, insert assertion-testing code into methods manually. If there is a possibility that you might want to turn off the assertion-testing code or exclude it from some configurations of your program, use the Conditional Compilation pattern.

When assertion-testing code detects that an assertion is false, it typically handles the failure by sending a report of the failure to `System.err` or an appropriate error logging mechanism. It then throws an unchecked exception.*

---

* Objects that are an instance of `RuntimeException`, `Error` or one of their subclasses are unchecked exceptions. A method's callers are not required to do anything to acknowledge the possibility that that method may throw an unchecked exception.

It is usual to report an unsatisfied precondition at runtime by throwing a checked exception.* If a method throws a checked exception, its callers are required to either catch the exception or declare that they throw the exception. Designing a method to throw a checked exception if its preconditions are not satisfied forces programmers that write calls to the method to devote some amount of thought to ensure that the method's preconditions are satisfied. It also forces them to take responsibility for what happens if the preconditions are not satisfied.

Unsatisfied postconditions and invariant conditions are usually reported by throwing unchecked exceptions. This is because satisfying them is the responsibility of the method and not its callers.

The type of exception to throw when a data condition is unsatisfied varies with the nature of the condition.

CONSEQUENCES

- If a sequence of events at runtime violates a method's contract, the assertion-testing code reports the violation and the sequence of events is aborted.
- Because you know which condition was violated and where it was violated, the time needed to track down and fix the source of the problem is greatly reduced.
- If assertion-testing code is no longer needed, it can easily be left out of the compiled version of the code.

IMPLEMENTATION

Manual insertion of code to test invariant conditions is awkward because invariant conditions apply to the entire duration of a method invocation. At minimum, invariant conditions should be tested at the beginning of a method and at all of its

---

* Throwable objects that are *not* instances of `RuntimeException`, `Error`, or one of their subclasses are checked exceptions.

exit points. Another place to consider testing invariant conditions is after code segments that modify something related to an invariant. If the method throws any checked exceptions, consider testing the invariants before the exception is thrown out of the method.

If the conditions of a method's contract are expressed in its code as assertions in specially formatted comments, a program such as a compiler or preprocessor can parse and in some way process the assertions. Such preprocessors are commercially available.

A mechanism that automatically detects discrepancies between a method's contract and its actual behavior can dramatically reduce the amount of time it takes to detect and fix bugs, as compared to finding discrepancies manually. Software to manage software testing in this way is also commercially available.

CODE EXAMPLE

Consider the following listing of a class called DateConstraint. Instances of this class specify constraints you can use to decide if a date is part of a set or not.

```
class DateConstraint {
    /**
     * @exception  InvalidConstraintException
     *             if the string that specifies the exception
     *             is not valid.
     */
    DateConstraint(String spec) throws InvalidConstraintException {
        ...
    } // constructor(String)
    ...
} // class DateConstraint
```

The preceding listing includes a constructor that takes a specification of dates as a string, parses the string, and initializes the DateConstraint object. The constraint has a precondition that the string passed to it be a syntactically valid date constraint. The constructor throws a InvalidConstraintException if this precondition is not satisfied. The InvalidConstraintException class is defined as a checked exception because callers of the constructor rely on the constructor to determine if the string contains a syntactically valid date constraint. This makes it part of the DateConstraint constructor's contract with its callers.

The following listing shows a method called getDatesInMonth that returns a list of the days in a month that satisfy a given specification. Like the constructor in the preceding listing, it has a precondition that the string passed to it be a syntactically valid date constraint. It delegates the enforcement of that condition to the DateConstraint class's constructor. The DateConstraint class's constructor also has a precondition that the string passed to it be a syntactically valid date constraint.

```
public List getDatesInMonth(int year, int month, String spec)
        throws InvalidConstraintException {
    // Parse date constraint specification.
    DateConstraint constraint;
    constraint = new DateConstraint(spec);
    // get dates from database
    ...
    if (dateList.size() > MAX_DAYS_IN_MONTH) {
        String err = "Got "+dateList.size()+" dates";
        throw new LogicException(err);
    } // if
    return dateList;
} // getDatesInMonth(int, int, String)
```

The getDatesInMonth method also has a postcondition. The postcondition is that the number of dates in the list that the method returns must be less than the number of days in the month. The method reports a violation of its postcondition by throwing a LogicException exception, which is defined as an unchecked exception. Like all postconditions, its violation indicates an internal programming error that the method's callers should not need to expect or anticipate. The following listing shows the definition of the LogicException class.

```
public class LogicException extends RuntimeException {
    private Throwable prevException;

    /**
     * Constructor.
     * @param msg The message associated with this exception.
     */
```

```
    public LogicException(String msg) {
        super(msg);
    } // constructor(String)


    /**
     * constructor
     * @param prev The thrown exception this is replacing.
     */
    public LogicException(Throwable prev) {
        prevException = prev;
    } // constructor(Throwable)


    /**
     * constructor
     * @param msg The message associated with this exception.
     * @param prev The thrown exception this is replacing.
     */
    public LogicException(String msg, Throwable prev) {
        super(msg);
        prevException = prev;
    } // constructor(Throwable)


    /**
     * Prints a stack trace of the exception
     * @param out The PrintStream to write the stack trace to.
     */
    public void printStackTrace(PrintStream out) {
        synchronized (out) {
            if (prevException != null) {
                out.print("ApplicationException: ");
                prevException.printStackTrace(out);
            } else {
                super.printStackTrace(out);
            } // if
        } // synchronized
    } // printStackTrace(PrintStream)
...
} // class LogicException
```

RELATED PATTERNS

Checked versus Unchecked Exceptions   The Checked versus
Unchecked Exceptions pattern explains reasons for using
unchecked exceptions to indicate assertion failures.

Conditional Compilation   You can use the Conditional
Compilation pattern with the Assertion Testing pattern to control whether assertion-testing code is included in a particular
configuration of a program.

Guaranteed Cleanup [Grand99]

SYNOPSIS

Ensure that internal data are in a consistent state if an operation is unable to execute to its normal completion. Ensure that external resources are in a consistent state and, if appropriate, are released after an operation is unable to execute to its normal completion.

CONTEXT

Suppose that you are writing a program that performs remote diagnostics on computers. The remote diagnostic program is supposed to connect to the computer to be tested, run some tests, and generate a diagnostic report. One of the things that can happen while the program runs the tests is that its connection to the computer under test can fail. Even if the connection fails, the program is required to generate a diagnostic report that shows the diagnostic information obtained up to the failure and records when it finished.

FORCES

- Some cleanup actions must be performed after an operation, regardless of whether the operation completes normally.
- The cleanup action must be performed immediately after the operation.
- Various cleanup mechanisms are triggered by the garbage collector, such as `finalize` methods and `ReferenceQueue` objects. These mechanisms are called when the garbage collector determines that an object is no longer alive. There is no limit to how long this can take. There is not even a guarantee that it will happen at all.

- The semantics of Java guarantee that the `finally` clause of a `try` statement will be executed unless the Java virtual machine that it runs on halts first.

SOLUTION

Use a `try` statement's `finally` clause to ensure that a cleanup action is performed after an operation terminates. Consider the following code listing, which satisfies the requirement specified under the "Context" heading:

```
public class DiagnosticHarness {
    /**
     * Run a sequence of diagnostic tests.
     * @param tests An iterator that returns the sequence of
     *              diagnostic test to be run.
     * @param connection The socket that connects the program to
     *                   the computer to be tested.
     * @param out A PrintStream to sent diagnostic output to.
     */
    public void runDiagnostic(Iterator tests,
                              Socket connection,
                              PrintStream out) throws IOException {
        out.print(new Date());
        out.println(": Beginning diagnostics.");
        try {
            while (tests.hasNext()) {
                ((DiagnosticTest)tests.next()).doIt(connection,
                                                    out);
            } // while
        } finally {
            out.print(new Date());
            out.println(": Diagnostics ended");
        } // try
    } // runDiagnostic(Iterator, Socket
} // class DiagnosticHarness
```

This method ensures that after the diagnostic tests have finished, no matter how they have finished, a message indicating when the diagnostics ended is appended to the report.

CONSEQUENCES

- Unless the Java virtual machine halts, the code in a `finally` clause will always be executed just before the flow of control would otherwise leave the `try` statement it is part of.

- A small amount of overhead is added.
- Putting cleanup code in the `finally` clause of a `try` statement can make a method more difficult to understand and to test because there will often be multiple execution paths that lead to the execution of the `finally` code. Some of the execution paths that lead to the execution of the `finally` code may not be obvious to someone reading the program or have been intended by the person who wrote the method.

For example, a method may be required to display a completion method when it finishes whatever it does. If the method has multiple `return` statements, code to display a completion message could be placed before each `return` statement. The person writing such a method may decide that it is better to write the message that displays the code once and put it in a `finally` clause, as is shown in the following listing.

```
public void doIt() {
    try {
        if (...) {
            ...
            return;
        } // if
        if (...) {
            ...
            return;
        } // if
        if (...) {
            ...
            return;
        } // if
        ...
    } finally {
        showStatus("operation complete");
    } // try
} // doIt()
```

In this listing, when any of the return statements are executed, the call to showStatus is executed. What is less obvious is that if a runtime exception, such as NullPointerException, is thrown from anywhere in the main try block, the call to showStatus is also executed. This execution path produces the "operation complete" message when the operation does not complete.

JAVA API USAGE

ObjectInputStream objects have a method named readObject that reconstructs an object from a stream of bytes that was written by an ObjectOutputStream object. The process of reconstructing an object from such a byte stream is called *deserializing* an object. Such byte streams usually contain objects and the objects that they refer to. The readObject method finishes deserializing the objects that an object refers to before it finishes with the object itself. Clearly, the readObject method must keep track of which object it is deserializing as it proceeds with an object, deserializes an object that it refers to, and then continues deserializing the first object.

The readObject method uses a finally clause to ensure that previously deserialized information about the object is restored when it is needed.

Maximize Privacy [Grand99]

SYNOPSIS

Make members of classes as private as possible.

CONTEXT

You want to make it as difficult as possible for maintenance programmers or people in other code-writing roles to create dependencies that are unintended by the program's design.

FORCES

- Class designs may leave the visibility of a class's methods or variables unspecified.
- When implementing a class specified in a design, the implementation may include methods and variables not specified in the design.
- If a variable or method is public, programmers can add code to any class that uses the variable or method.
- Programmers who do not understand the design of a set of classes may create dependencies between classes that are contrary to the intention of the design.
- Programmers cannot mistakenly create dependencies from classes in other packages that are contrary to the intent of the design if a class is not public. If a method or field is not public, then there is a smaller set of classes from which programmers can mistakenly create dependencies that are contrary to the intent of the design. If a method or field is private, programmers cannot create dependencies on it from anywhere outside its class.
- If a method that may be usefully called by other classes is declared private, an opportunity for reuse may be lost.

SOLUTION

If the visibility of a method or field is not specified by a design, or if a method or field is an implementation detail, its visibility should be as private as possible.

CONSEQUENCES

Making classes and their members as private as possible minimizes the opportunities for programmers to add dependencies that are contrary to the design.

JAVA API USAGE

Very consistently, throughout the implementation of Java's core API, classes that are not documented as part of the API are not public. Members of public classes that are not documented as part of the API are not public.

CODE EXAMPLE

This example is based on an already implemented class named Queue. This class implements a queue data structure. It has two public methods. Its push method adds a given object to the beginning of a queue. Its pull method removes an object from the end of a queue and returns it.

The design in Figure 8.1 shows the Queue class and some classes that extend the Queue class. The additional classes extend the Queue class in a way described in the discussion of the Decorator pattern in Volume 1. The QueueWrapper class provides implementations of the push and pull methods that simply delegate to another Queue object. Though not very useful in itself, it simplifies the implementation of wrapper classes for Queue with additional functionality as subclasses of the QueueWrapper class. The code example considered here is the implementation of the QueueWrapper class.

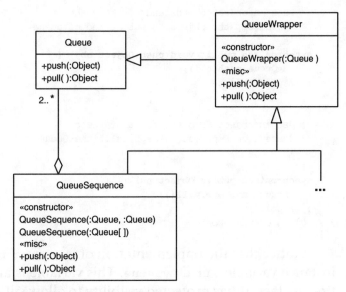

FIGURE 8.1 Queue wrapper classes.

The design does not specify the visibility for the QueueWrapper class's constructor. You will want it to be possible to instantiate subclasses of the QueueWrapper class, so its only constructor cannot be private. To make the QueueWrapper class as useful as possible, you would like it to be possible for subclasses of QueueWrapper to be part of any package. This means that the constructor cannot have package visibility. However, protected visibility is sufficient for the constructor since there is no need for arbitrary classes to be able to access it.

The following listing shows the implementation of the QueueWrapper class:

```
public abstract class QueueWrapper {
    protected Queue myQueue;      // The queue wrapped by this object

    /**
     * constructor.
     * @param aQueue The Queue to be wrapped by this object.
     */
    protected QueueWrapper(Queue aQueue) {
        myQueue = aQueue;
    } // constructor(Queue)

    /**
```

```
      * Puts an object on the end of the queue
      * @param obj the object to put at end of queue
      */
     synchronized public void push(Object obj) {
         myQueue.push(obj);
     } // push(Object)

     /**
      * Get an object from the front of the queue
      * @exception EmptyQueueException If the Queue
      * is empty.
      */
     synchronized public Object pull() {
         return myQueue.pull();
     } // pull()
} // class QueueWrapper
```

Notice that the implementation of QueueWrapper includes an instance variable called myQueue. This variable is an implementation artifact. It has protected visibility to allow subclasses of the QueueWrapper class to manipulate its value but not allow unrelated classes to access it.

Also, consider the following listing of the Queue class:

```
public class Queue {
    private Vector vector = new Vector();

    /**
     * Put an object on the end of the queue
     * @param obj the object to put at end of queue
     */
    synchronized public void push(Object obj) {
        vector.addElement(obj);
    } // push(Object)

    /**
     * Get an object from the front of the queue
     * @exception EmptyQueueException If the Queue
     * is empty.
     */
    synchronized public Object pull() {
        if (vector.size() == 0)
          throw new EmptyQueueException();
        Object obj = vector.elementAt(0);
        vector.removeElementAt(0);
        return obj;
    } // pull()
} // class Queue
```

The `Queue` class has an instance variable named `vector`. This instance variable is an implementation artifact. It has private visibility because there is no need for any other class to access it.

RELATED PATTERNS

Low Coupling/High Cohesion   The Low Coupling/High Cohesion pattern also tries to avoid dependencies between classes.

Return New Objects from Accessor Method [Gold97]

SYNOPSIS

Accessor methods return values or objects that indicate an object's state. If the objects that an accessor method returns are mutable, they should be copies rather than the actual state that determines objects. This prevents changes to the returned object from also changing the state of the accessor method's associated object.

CONTEXT

Suppose that you are implementing a class called CalendarEvent that describes events scheduled in a personal calendar. The UML description of CalendarEvent appears in Figure 8.2.

The CalendarEvent class's setTime method sets the start and end times of an event object by setting its start and end variables. It is responsible for ensuring that the start time is not after the end time. The getStartTime method returns a CalendarEvent object's start time as a Date object. If you simply implement it by returning the Date object that is the value of the CalendarEvent

```
CalendarEvent

-start:Date
-end:Date
...

+getDescription( ):String
+setDescription(:String)
+getStartTime( ):Date
+getEndTime( ):Date
+setTime(start:Date,
end:Date)
...
```

FIGURE 8.2 UML description of CalendarEvent.

object's `start` variable, you compromise the integrity of the `CalendarEvent` class.

The problem is that after the `getStartTime` method returns the `Date` object that determines a `CalendarEvent` object's start time, the method's caller is free to change the content of the `Date` object.

FORCES

- A class has an accessor method that returns an object that determines the state of an instance of the class.
- The object that the accessor method returns is mutable. In other words, it is possible for other objects to modify the object that the accessor method returns.
- There is no reasonable way to redesign the class so that it does not expose its internal state. Such redesigns usually involve reassigning the responsibilities of classes.
- A class must prevent the state of its instances from being directly modified by other classes. To ensure the integrity of its instances, other classes must be forced to work through the methods that the class provides for modifying the state of its instances.

SOLUTION

Some objects have associated objects that determine their state. An object's accessor methods should never return one of the associated state-determining objects if it is mutable—its contents can be changed. Instead, accessor methods should return copies of such state-determining objects.

CONSEQUENCES

- The integrity of an object's encapsulation is maintained when its accessor methods return copies of mutable state-determining objects rather than the state-determining objects themselves, so long as changes to the copies do not affect the original objects.

■ This pattern adds the time and memory overhead needed to create copies of objects.

IMPLEMENTATION

All Java classes inherit a method from the `Object` class called `clone`. An object's `clone` method returns a copy of the object. Unfortunately, the `clone` method has protected visibility. This means that unless an object is an array, instances of unrelated classes cannot call the object's `clone` method to copy the object.

Some classes provide other ways to copy an object. For example, the following method returns a copy of a given `Vector` object:

```
public static Vector copyVector(Vector v) {
    Vector newVector = new Vector(v.size());
    newVector.addAll(v);
    return newVector;
} // copyVector(Vector)
```

JAVA API USAGE

Instances of the `java.text.MessageFormat` class use an array of `Format` objects. The class has a method called `getFormats` that returns an array of the `Format` objects that a `MessageFormat` object uses. The array that it returns is not the array that the `MessageFormat` object uses, but a copy of the array.

CODE EXAMPLE

The following listing shows part of the implementation of the `CalendarEvent` class discussed under the "Context" heading. As you read it, notice that its accessor methods do not return the actual `Date` objects that determine the event's start and end. Instead, they return a copy of those `Date` objects.

```
                public class CalendarEvent {
                    private Date start;
                    private Date end;
...
                    /**
                     * Set the start and end time of this event.
                     * @param start This event's start time.
                     * @param end This event's end time.
                     * @exception IllegalArgumentException
                     *                if end is before start.
                     */
                    public void setTime(Date start, Date end) {
                        if (end.before(start)) {
                            String msg = "end before start";
                            throw new IllegalArgumentException(msg);
                        } // if
                        ...
                    } // setTime(Date, Date)

                    /**
                     * Return this event's start time.
                     */
                    public Date getStart() {
                        return copyDate(start);
                    } // getStart()

                    /**
                     * Return this event's end time.
                     */
                    public Date getEnd() {
                        return copyDate(end);
                    } // getEnd()

                    private Date copyDate(Date d) {
                        return new Date(d.getTime());
                    } // copyDate(Date)
                } // class CalendarEvent
```

RELATED PATTERNS

Copy Mutable Parameters   The Return New Objects from
   Accessor Method pattern avoids the situation of an object that
   shares its state-determining objects with callers of its accessor
   methods. The Copy Mutable Parameters pattern avoids a similar situation with callers that pass state-determining objects
   into its constructors and methods.

Copy Mutable Parameters [Pryce98]

SYNOPSIS

Objects may be passed to a method or constructor that is used to determine the state of its associated object. If the passed objects are mutable, copies of them should be used to determine the object's state, rather than the original passed object. This prevents changes to the passed object from also changing the state of the object associated with the method or constructor.

CONTEXT

Suppose that you are implementing a class called `CalendarEvent` that describes events scheduled in a personal calendar. The UML description of `CalendarEvent` appears in Figure 8.2.

The `CalendarEvent` class's `setTime` method sets the start and end times of a calendar event object by setting its `start` and `end` variables. It is responsible for ensuring that the start time is not after the end time. If the `setTime` method simply sets the `CalendarEvent` object's `start` and `end` variables to refer to the `Date` objects passed to it, the integrity of the `CalendarEvent` class is compromised.

The problem is that after it passes `Date` objects to the `setTime` method, the caller of the `setTime` method is free to change the content of the `Date` objects.

FORCES

- A class has a method or constructor that is passed an object whose content is used to determine the state of an instance of the class.
- The objects that will be passed to the method or constructor are mutable. In other words, it is possible for the caller of

the method or constructor to modify the content of the object after calling the method or constructor.

■ A class must prevent the state of its instances from being directly modified by other classes. Other classes must work through the methods that the class provides for modifying the state of its instances.

SOLUTION

Methods that are passed arguments that determine the state of their associated object should not directly assign such an argument to an instance variable if the argument is a mutable object. Instead, they should assign a copy of the argument to the instance variable.

CONSEQUENCES

■ The integrity of an object's encapsulation is maintained when its methods assign copies of argument objects to instance variables, rather than assigning the argument objects themselves.

■ This pattern adds the time and memory overhead needed to create copies of objects.

IMPLEMENTATION

All Java classes inherit a method from the Object class called clone. An object's clone method returns a copy of the object. Unfortunately, the clone method has protected visibility. This means that unless an object is an array, instances of unrelated classes cannot call the object's clone method to copy the object.

Some classes provide other ways to copy an object. For example, the following method returns a copy of a given Vector object:

```
public static Vector copyVector(Vector v) {
    Vector newVector = new Vector(v.size());
    newVector.addAll(v);
```

```
        return newVector;
    } // copyVector(Vector)
```

JAVA API USAGE

Instances of the `java.text.MessageFormat` class use an array of
`Format` objects. The class has a method called `setFormats` that
sets the array of `Format` objects that a `MessageFormat` object uses.
The array passed into the method is not the array that the
`MessageFormat` object uses. Instead, it uses a copy of it.

CODE EXAMPLE

The following listing shows part of the implementation of the
`CalendarEvent` class discussed under the "Context" heading. As
you read it, notice that its `setTime` method does not set the `start`
and `end` instance variables to the actual `Date` objects passed into
it. Instead, it assigns a copy of those `Date` objects to the instance
variables.

```
public class CalendarEvent {
    private Date start;
    private Date end;
    ...
    /**
     * Set the start and end time of this event.
     * @param start This event's start time.
     * @param end This event's end time.
     * @exception IllegalArgumentException
     *                if end is before start.
     */
    public void setTime(Date start, Date end) {
        if (end.before(start)) {
            String msg = "end before start";
            throw new IllegalArgumentException(msg);
        } // if
        this.start = copyDate(start);
        this.end = copyDate(end);
    } // setTime(Date, Date)
    ...
    private Date copyDate(Date d) {
        return new Date(d.getTime());
    } // copyDate(Date)
} // class CalendarEvent
```

RELATED PATTERNS

Return New Objects from Accessor Method   The Copy Mutable Parameters pattern avoids the situation of an object that shares its state-determining objects with callers of its methods that specify those objects. The Return New Objects from Accessor Method pattern avoids a similar situation with callers of methods that return state-determining objects.

9

Testing Patterns

The patterns in this chapter describe different methods of testing software. Testing software involves executing the software under controlled conditions to see if its behavior is consistent with a set of expectations.

The software-testing patterns described in this chapter vary with the granularity of the tested software—individual classes, groups of classes, or entire programs—the purpose of the test, and the thoroughness of the test.

Black Box Testing [Grand99]

Black Box Testing is also known as *Functional Testing* or *Closed Box Testing*.

SYNOPSIS

Ensure that software meets requirements by designing tests based solely on requirements. Do not base tests on the manner in which the software is implemented.

CONTEXT

Suppose you have a contract to develop software. The contract includes very detailed requirements that describe what the software should and should not do. You will receive payment for the software only if it satisfies all of the contractual requirements.

You have quality concerns for the product that go beyond the requirements. You are concerned about how the program will behave when the size of one of its inputs reaches the size of one of its internal buffers. You are concerned that large input values will overflow the data type used to represent those values internally.

These are valid concerns. However, your overriding concern is to receive payment. For this reason, you decide that your software testing will be based on the requirements and not on any of the software's implementation details. Later on, if there is time, you will expand the scope of your testing.

Testing software in a manner that is not based on any knowledge of the software's implementation or internal structure is called *black box testing*.

FORCES

- You must ensure that the software works in a way that satisfies a set of specifications. The specifications indicate what the software must and must not do.
- The number of combinations of specified tasks that a program must perform is usually large.
- In addition to ensuring that the software will work as specified, you want to ensure that it will perform correctly in all situations. The good news is that it is not necessary to test the software under every situation, only under those situations that can possibly make a difference. The bad news is that the number of situations that can make a difference is proportionate to the number of execution paths through the software. This can make the cost of extending the scope of testing beyond what is required by the specifications prohibitive.
- You choose to compromise on the scope of your testing by designing it to test only specified behaviors and not basing any testing on the internal structure of the software.

SOLUTION

Design tests for software based on the requirements for that software. The designs for tests in a black box test suite will typically include the following information:

- The requirements that motivate each test.
- A list of the resources used by the software and their expected state prior to each test. The list can include the state of a database or the values of environment variables, but only if they are part of the software's documented operating specification.
- The inputs that will be provided to the software during the test.
- The expected outputs from the software and the expected final states of the resources used by the software.

CONSEQUENCES

- You can ensure that the software satisfies its requirements.
- Your testing program will focus on those tests that provide the most immediate return on the investment.
- Your testing program will be far from exhaustive and will not be sufficient for life-critical applications.

CODE EXAMPLE

Suppose you have the task of designing a suite of black box tests to test an applet. The applet has one requirement: When the user enters three numbers and presses a button, the applet will tell the user if those numbers are possible lengths of the sides of a triangle.

For such a simple program, the tests will be simple. The software has only one stated requirement. There is no explicitly required initial state. There is one implicit requirement for the initial state that is shared by all applets—that it be possible for a browser or other applet-hosting environment to launch the applet. Since any test of the applet will implicitly test this requirement, the test specifications do not explicitly include any mention of it.

You design the first test case to directly test the program's requirement. The test will consist of entering the numbers 3, 4, and 5, and then pressing the button. The expected outcome is that the applet will indicate that those numbers can be the lengths of the sides of a triangle.

You can infer additional requirements from knowledge of the problem domain. In order to be the lengths of the sides of a triangle, each of the three numbers must be less than the sum of the other two. In other words, if a, b, and c are the three numbers, they can be the lengths of the sides of a triangle if and only if all of the following is true:

$$a + b > c$$
$$b + c > a$$
$$a + c > b$$

Based on this inferred requirement, you design tests to violate the requirement with the expectation that the program will recognize that numbers such as 3, 8, and 22 cannot be the lengths of the sides of a triangle.

Another requirement that you can infer is that all three numbers must be greater than 0, so you design tests to verify that the program rejects numbers that are less than or equal to 0.

Because you are designing test cases for black box testing, there are some test cases that you will not consider. For example, you expect that if the numbers given to the program are too large, they will exceed the range of numbers that the program's internal number representation can handle. Though you expect that the program will produce an error message in that case rather than give the wrong answer, you don't design tests, because you would need to know what data type the program uses to represent the numbers in order to select the numbers to use in the test case.

RELATED PATTERNS

White Box Testing White box testing is the complement of black box testing. It involves designing test cases based on the internal structure of the software to be tested.

White Box Testing [Grand99]

White Box Testing is also known as *Clear Box Testing.*

SYNOPSIS

Design a suite of tests to exhaustively test software by testing it in all meaningful situations. The set of meaningful situations is determined from knowledge of the software's internal structure. A complete set of tests will exercise all possible execution paths through the software.

CONTEXT

Suppose you are developing software for a space probe's navigational computer. The software must be free of defects, since an incorrect computer direction at the wrong time could cause the probe to be irrecoverably lost in space and result in complete mission failure.

To ensure that the software is free of defects, it is not sufficient to test it against its requirements. You need to ensure that it operates correctly under all conditions. To accomplish this, you do not actually have to test the software under all combinations of conditions. Many combinations of conditions will test the software in exactly the same way. You need information about the software's internal structure to determine which tests are necessary and meaningful.

FORCES

- You must ensure that the software works in a manner that satisfies a set of specifications for what the software must and must not do.

- In addition to ensuring that the software will work as specified, you must ensure that it will perform correctly in all situations.
- Using knowledge of the internal structure of the software, it is possible to ensure that the software will work in all situations without testing it in all situations.
- The minimum amount of testing that is required to ensure that the software will work in all conditions must exercise all possible execution paths through the software.
- Careful analysis of the boundary conditions involved in each execution path can reduce the number of tests required to adequately exercise an execution path from the number of possible values that can flow through that execution path to just a handful.

SOLUTION

Design tests for software based on the requirements for that software and on its internal structure. The test designs for a white box test suite will typically include the following information:

- The test name.
- The requirements that motivate the test.
- The expected state, prior to the test, of the resources used by the software. This can include such things as the state of a database, the values of environment variables, or limits on available resources (such as memory or disk space). It can also specify minimum demands that will be placed on a program, such as the number of simulated concurrent users.
- The inputs that will be provided to the software during the test.
- Any specific execution paths that the test is supposed to exercise.
- Boundary conditions that the test exercises.
- The expected outputs from the software and the expected final state of the resources that the software uses.

A *boundary condition* is a condition that changes if a value is above or below a given value. Some examples of common boundary conditions are:

- Values that cause a numeric data type to overflow
- Values that cause a data structure to overflow
- Values that cause the boolean expression in an `if` condition to be true or false

To ensure that you test all execution paths through the software, use a coverage analysis tool that keeps track of which execution paths have been tested.

CONSEQUENCES

- You can ensure that the software satisfies its requirements.
- Your testing program will focus on ensuring that the software works correctly under all conditions.
- A white box testing program can be very expensive. It typically involves an enormous number of tests that require a great amount of labor to create and require a great amount of time to run, unless they can be run on a large server farm.

CODE EXAMPLE

Returning to the space probe navigational computer discussed under the "Context" heading, you find that you have a test suite that covers all of the probe's formal requirements. You extend this by embarking on a white box testing program.

A key part of any white box testing program is tracking what execution paths a test suite exercises through the software. You can use a tool called a *coverage analyzer* to keep track of the execution paths that your test suite exercises.

You begin by examining the existing tests' execution paths to determine what boundary conditions apply to them. You design two common types of tests in this manner:

1. Tests that involve input values outside the range that an internal data representation can handle
2. Tests that supply just enough data to fill up an internal data buffer and tests that supply one more piece of data than an internal buffer can hold

In addition to exploring the execution paths of existing tests, you will create additional tests to exercise all of the remaining possible execution paths and their boundary conditions.

RELATED PATTERNS

Black Box Testing   Black box testing is the complement of white box testing. It involves designing tests based only on the specifications of the software to be tested.

Unit Testing   Because there are many fewer execution paths through an individual class than there are through an entire program, it is more common to apply white box testing to unit testing than to testing larger pieces of software.

Unit testing may be able to exercise execution paths in classes that are currently unavailable in the environment for which you are developing software. Exercising those execution paths avoids future surprises.

Unit Testing [Grand99]

SYNOPSIS

Test individual classes in isolation from the other classes of the program under development.

CONTEXT

You are managing a group of programmers on a project. In order to ensure that your programmers focus on what they know best, you make sure that one programmer has the primary responsibility for each class of the software that you are developing. You expect to get a few benefits from this strategy. One benefit is that less overall time will be spent on debugging because each programmer will be able to focus on debugging his or her own code.

After this policy has been in place for a while, you notice that it is not working as you had expected. Your programmers are still spending an inordinate amount of time tracking down bugs in classes for which other programmers are responsible. To solve this problem, you set a new policy requiring the programmers to test each class in isolation before they check it into the shared code base.

FORCES

- You don't want programmers to spend their time tracking the source of a bug down to a specific class.
- When programmers test an individual class in isolation, they do not have to determine which class is the source of a bug.
- Most classes are not designed to operate in isolation.
- When classes are tested in isolation, it is possible to test them under conditions or combinations of conditions that

they will not be subjected to within the program for which they are being developed.

SOLUTION

Programmers test each class in isolation before checking it in. The designs for such tests typically include:

- Name of the test
- Test objectives, including the execution paths and boundary conditions being tested
- Description of the test
- Expected state, prior to the test, of the resources used by the software; may include the state of a database or the values of environment variables
- Test initialization procedures
- Test inputs
- Procedure for running the test
- Expected test results

To implement a unit test, you have to write a driver class to set up the test environment and call the methods of the tested class. You may also have to write stub classes to simulate the behavior of classes that are not part of the test.

CONSEQUENCES

- Programmers spend less time tracking down bugs.
- There is more time to fix bugs.
- Unit testing allows a class to be tested in situations that it may not be possible to create when the class is used as part of the program for which it is being developed. This makes it possible to detect bugs in the class that will not be expressed in the behavior of the program of which it is a part. There are two benefits of detecting such bugs:

1. Future maintenance programmers may modify the program in a way that causes such bugs to be expressed. By detecting such bugs through unit testing, you ensure that future maintenance programmers will not have to spend time tracking down bugs in classes they did not modify. This is also an additional reason for doing white box testing at the unit-testing level.

2. Thorough unit testing of a class improves its reusability. Thorough white box unit testing of a class ensures that it can be reused without stopping to track down previously undetected bugs.

■ Constructing tests for a class in isolation may present some challenges. Most classes have dependencies on other classes. To truly test a class in isolation, you must test it without relying on any of the other classes that you have under development. This means that your test environment can use other classes that are not under development and of whose behavior you are confident. However, it also means that you will need dummy versions of all the classes under development upon which the class under testing depends. The dummy versions should have stubbed implementations of the class methods that perform adequately enough for successful testing.

The reason for using dummy classes is that it will generally take much less time to ensure that they are correct. Once you know that they are correct, the time spent testing can be focused entirely on the class that is the subject of the test.

In some cases, the amount of functionality that related classes must have in order to be useful in testing makes the construction of dummy classes impractical. There are some alternatives.

Suppose you want to unit test a class named A. The A class is dependent on another class named B. It is not feasible to create a dummy version of the B class. However, the B class has no dependency on the A class. If the B class is unit tested independently of the A class, it can be acceptable to use the actual B class for unit testing, rather than a dummy version.

If a class to be unit tested and another class are mutually dependent and it is not feasible to create a dummy version of the other class, consider unit testing the two classes together.

■ Tools that help you understand the dependencies between classes are very helpful in planning unit tests.

RELATED PATTERNS

System Testing   System testing is a complement to unit testing. System testing involves testing an entire program rather than individual classes.

White Box Testing   White box testing is more often used at the unit-testing level than at larger levels of granularity. This is because there are fewer combinations of execution paths to consider at the unit-testing level. Also, white box testing at the unit level makes it easier to reuse classes and lowers long-term software maintenance costs.

Integration Testing [Grand99]

SYNOPSIS

Test individually developed classes together for the first time.

CONTEXT

You are developing a nontrivial piece of software. You write and unit test each class. You then put the classes together so that they will collectively function as a program. The exercise of putting classes together for the first time and making them work together is called *integration testing*. You find many problems that are difficult to track down because it is difficult to determine which class is the cause. You conclude that you need a better plan.

FORCES

- No matter how precisely you specify a set of classes, or how thoroughly you unit test them, you do not know that they will work together as intended until you test them together.
- Throwing all of a program's classes together to be tested at once is called *big bang* integration testing. Big bang integration can be very chaotic unless there are relatively few classes in a program.
- The individual classes to be integrated rarely become available for integration at exactly the same time and they usually do not become available exactly when scheduled.
- When you use big bang integration testing, you do not do any integration testing until all of your classes are written, which can result in the inefficient use of your programmers' time, especially in a team environment. This can leave some programmers idle until integration testing begins.

- You can minimize the chaos of integration testing and make scheduling easier for programmers by initially testing a few classes together and gradually increasing the number of classes in a progressive manner.
- In order to make progressive integration testing work, you will need to substitute driver and stub classes for the classes that are not yet integrated.
- When you devise a plan for progressive integration testing, you will need to choose an order in which to add and combine classes into the test. You can choose a reasonable order more easily by following the structure of a program than by inventing arbitrary groupings.
- Your strategy for selecting classes to test should be flexible, since classes may not become available for testing in the expected order.
- The goal of integration testing is to ensure that individually developed classes work together. Trying to run a comprehensive suite of tests at this point to verify that the program satisfies its requirements is not appropriate, since most of the integration testing will be done without the participation of the full set of classes.
- Matching the tests that you run to the order in which you include classes in integration tests is the most efficient way to perform integration testing. Tests that exercise the core functionality of just the integrated classes waste the least amount of time on unavailable functionality.

SOLUTION

When you design an integration-testing plan, first decide on a facet of the program's structure that you will use to organize the testing. Some common methods to determine this are:

- Incorporate classes in a top-down or bottom-up pattern, or some combination of the two. This technique is easy to understand at a conceptual level, but may be difficult to apply to most object-oriented designs. The problem is that most object-oriented designs are not very hierarchical.

- Incorporate clusters of classes that are related to a common program feature or use case.
- Incorporate classes that are related to a common thread.

Once you have decided how you will organize your integration testing, begin writing driver and stub classes accordingly. The driver classes are responsible for setting the environment for a test and calling the methods of classes under test. Stub classes masquerade as classes on which the classes under test have dependencies. However, stub classes provide little or no functionality and exist solely to satisfy dependencies during a test.

The actual tests performed during integration testing should exercise the basic functionality of the classes under test. However, exhaustive testing at this point may not be useful. You should merely try to test the most basic functionality of each class to ensure that the classes will work well enough with each other to move on to system testing.

Integration testing for small to medium-sized projects is often done with less formal planning than other types of testing because there is less need to repeat it. Once a large enough set of classes is integrated, it may never be necessary to test those classes in that mode again. Future integration testing would then be performed only on other groups of classes.

Integration testing for larger projects requires more formal planning. A more formal approach is required when multiple development groups are involved in integration testing. Each group is typically responsible for a different set of classes. This gives rise to a higher level of organization for integration testing. Each group will generally perform integration testing for the group of classes for which it is responsible, because it will be most familiar with those classes.

When it comes time to perform integration testing on multiple groups of classes from multiple development groups, it will be necessary to involve people in the integration testing who are not familiar with all of the classes being tested. In such situations, a formal plan to instruct everyone involved on how to run the tests and what to expect from them is invaluable.

CONSEQUENCES

- Integration testing can detect bugs arising from incompatibilities between classes that unit testing cannot easily detect.
- It generally takes less time to track down bugs that you find during integration testing than if you catch them later, during system testing.
- It generally takes more time to track down bugs that you find during integration testing than if you catch them sooner, during unit testing.

RELATED PATTERNS

System Testing   Integration testing generally involves smaller groups of classes than are tested during system testing. Consider integration testing as an activity that allows you to make a smooth transition from the phase in development when it is impractical to use a test larger than a unit test to the phase when it is possible to run systems tests on most of a program's features.

Unit Testing   Unit testing involves individual classes or very small groups of classes. System testing involves larger groups of classes.

System Testing [Grand99]

SYNOPSIS

Test a program as a whole entity, in an environment similar to the one in which it is intended to run, to ensure that it conforms to its specifications.

CONTEXT

After all the pieces of a program have been written, unit tested, and put through integration testing, you still need to ensure that the program as a whole satisfies all of its requirements and matches its other specifications. This requires a comprehensive testing program.

FORCES

- Some software defects become apparent only when an entire program is tested. Some defects manifest themselves only in some but not all of the environments and circumstances in which a program is required to work.
- You must verify that a program conforms to its specifications and satisfies its formal requirements.
- You want to ensure that a program's performance matches the documentation.
- Program requirements are not usually precise enough to require that a program be implemented in a specific way. Such requirements can allow different interpretations of what a program should do. Such ambiguity increases the difficulty of system testing, since it implies that more than one behavior for the program is acceptable in some situations. If a program exhibits different but acceptable behaviors in the

same situation, all of those behaviors should be treated as correct.

- A program's complete set of requirements will usually be too complicated to understand all at once. Also, it is generally not practical to test all of a program's requirements with a single test case.

- Organizing a program's requirements into sufficiently small logical groups allows you to understand entire groups of requirements at once and allows you to design focused test cases that exercise all or most of a group of requirements.

- System testing can involve a tremendous number of tests. It is difficult to know how to manage a large number of test cases without an explicitly stated master plan that guides the overall system-testing process. Such a plan can provide guidelines for such things as:

  - The point in the development process when system testing should begin

  - Priorities to use in deciding which test cases to design and run first

  - Conditions under which system testing should be aborted without completing all tests

- The large number of tests that need to be run during system testing can make manual analysis of the test results very time consuming.

- Creating automated tests for programs that receive commands or data through a GUI is more complicated than just putting data in a file. It usually involves assumptions about the layout of a GUI on a screen, the internal organization of a GUI, or both.

SOLUTION

When you design and implement a complete set of tests for system testing, begin by formulating a master system-testing plan. The elements of a master system-testing plan should include the following:

The point in the development process when system testing should begin.   This will typically be at a point in development when enough of a program's core features are working to make system testing useful. Early in the development of a program, none of its features will work. A substantial amount of time may pass before enough of a program's infrastructure is built to make it possible to test any of its features in the way that they will be used when the program is complete. Only when this is possible does it make sense to begin system testing. This is the part of the plan where you work out the details of shifting from integration testing to system testing.

A master plan for system testing should define the infrastructure and features of a program that must be implemented before system testing can start.

Priorities to use in deciding which test cases to design and run first.   There will usually be feature-based priorities. There may be some features that must work before you can begin testing other features. Arrange your development schedule to address these features first. Features on which no other feature depends can be tested last.

For example, suppose you are developing a word processor. A very fundamental feature of a word processor is that the user must be able to add characters to a document by typing on a keyboard. Since many other features depend on this feature working properly, this feature should be available and tested very early during system testing. If spell checking is a feature on which no other features depend, then it can be tested toward the end of system testing.

Other priorities may come into play due to non-feature-based requirements, such as deadlines.

Conditions under which system testing should be aborted without completing all tests.   When you develop your priorities for designing tests, you will determine dependency relationships between the tests.

You can then base system-testing priorities on these dependencies. You can also use these dependencies to determine when tests should not be run.

Tests that will not run successfully if another test fails should not be run if that test fails, since running them is a waste of effort. Also, to avoid spending an excessive amount of time running tests that fail, you may decide to abort a system test altogether if too many tests fail.

When you organize the dependencies and priorities for a master system-testing plan, it is helpful to first organize the program's requirements and specifications into logical groupings.

The suite of tests you design for system testing must include tests for all of the situations and environments in which a program is required to operate. The variations you must account for may include:

- Different operating platforms.
- Different program configurations.
- Different startup environments and launching mechanisms.
- Recovery from various failure modes. It may be particularly important to focus on failure modes that result when a resource is exhausted. Failure modes such as insufficient memory or disk space are often not accounted for in designs or their implementations.
- Different levels of load on the program and different amounts of contention by other programs for the same resources.

The design of individual tests should focus on specific software requirements and specifications. The designs for such tests typically include:

- Name of the test.
- Test objectives, including the requirements and specifications being tested.
- Description of the test.

- Expected state, prior to the test, of the resources used by the program; may include such things as the state of a database or the amount of available memory.
- Any additional procedures required to initialize the test. For example, it may be necessary to issue some commands to a program just to put it in the state that is to be tested. For example, if you are designing a test for the spell-check feature of a word processor, you might specify that the word processor must be told to open a particular document before the actual test of the spell checker may begin.
- Data required to run the test.
- Procedure for running the test.
- Expected test results.

Because of the large number of tests that you must typically run during system testing, it is common practice to build software to automate running the tests and analyzing the test results. This test automation software is called a *test harness*. Such software typically will:

- Ensure that all resources needed for a test are in their expected state. For example, the test harness may run a script that creates an empty database and fills it with specified test data.
- Start the program and feed it commands from a script. If the program takes its commands from a GUI, the test harness should include a facility for sending recorded or scripted keystrokes and mouse events to a GUI.
- Capture the program's output in a file. If applicable, the test harness should also capture screen snapshots at appropriate points.
- Compare the captured output and screen snapshots from the test with expected output and screen snapshots. If there are no unexpected discrepancies, the test harness should report that the test has succeeded. If there are unexpected discrepancies, it should report that the test has failed and identify the unexpected discrepancies.

Expected discrepancies will include things that are expected to be different with every run of the test. For example, if the program displays a screen with the current time, that part of the screen will be different every time the test is run.

- Ensure that tests whose success is dependent on the successful completion of other tests are not run if those tests are not successful.

Products are available that can be used as major building blocks for building a test harness, so the effort should involve relatively little, low-level programming.

CONSEQUENCES

- System testing allows you to achieve as much confidence that a program will satisfy its requirements and specifications as you have the time and money to achieve.
- Defining preconditions for the start of system testing allows you to more accurately incorporate system testing into a development schedule. The preconditions make it possible to determine some dependency relationships between system testing and other tasks in a schedule.
- Defining preconditions for running individual tests minimizes wasted effort.
- In a system of substantial complexity, the cost of exhaustive system testing for a software program can exceed the cost of designing and writing the software. For this reason, most software is not exhaustively system tested unless it is of a life-critical nature.

    One way to keep the effort required for system testing down is to keep the design of the program simple. If there is only one way for a feature to function, only one test is needed to verify that it functions accordingly.* For example, a clock that always displays the time in the same mode requires only one test case. If the clock is enhanced to allow the user to

---

* Additional testing may be required if there are nonfunctional requirements, such as performance requirements.

select different time display modes, then each mode must be tested, along with the mechanism for selecting the mode.
- Using a test harness ensures that tests will be run in a consistent manner, which makes the results more reproducible.

RELATED PATTERNS

Integration Testing   Integration testing ensures that the software being tested is in a sufficiently functional state that it is possible to run groups of system tests and get meaningful results.

Regression Testing   Regression testing allows you to use system tests to monitor the progress of programmers and measure the overall conformance of the software to its requirements and specifications.

Regression Testing [Grand99]

SYNOPSIS

Keep track of the outcome of software testing with a suite of tests over time. This allows you to monitor the completion of coding as programmers make incremental changes. It allows you to determine if a change to a program has introduced new bugs.

CONTEXT

When programmers are writing code to implement a design, a good way to track their progress is to keep track of when features first begin working.

Later in the project, programmers may spend more time fixing bugs than implementing features. At this stage, you can better measure progress by tracking two things at the end of each day:

1. Increase in number of features that work compared to number that previously did not
2. Decrease in number of features that don't work compared to number that previously did

FORCES

- Running a suite of tests after changing code in a program may be sufficient to tell you if a change in the code has had the desired effect.
- Running a suite of tests is not sufficient to tell you if a change in the code has had any undesired effects, because it does not give you a way to tell if anything about the program has changed. It simply allows you to determine if the current behavior meets your expectations based on the change.

- When you are managing a group of programmers who are writing a new program or new features for an existing program, you need a way to track their progress.
- Requiring programmers to write very detailed progress reports is not a good use of their time. Piecing together the details of all the programmers' progress reports to form an overall picture of their progress can be time consuming and can produce inconsistent results.
- An automated tracking system that reports programmers' progress in a consistent way can save time for workers and manager alike, in addition to providing more consistent results.

SOLUTION

After you make a change to the software, run all the appropriate tests that you have and record the results, keeping track of which tests the software passes and which it fails. If the suite of tests you run includes tests that exercise the changes made to the software, the test results will tell you if the changes have had their desired effect.

Comparing the results of the most recent test with the results of a previous test will tell you if any tests that passed the previous test run have failed in the most recent, which will point out any undesired effects of the software changes.

If you are making changes to a program on an occasional basis, it is reasonable to do regression testing on an equally occasional basis, after each change is applied. Occasional changes are typical during the maintenance portion of the software life cycle.

During the coding portion of the software life cycle, changes are typically made on a continuing and ongoing basis. It is not practical to perform regression testing after every change is applied to the program. A common solution is to run regression on a nightly basis.

CONSEQUENCES

- Regression testing provides a way to track progress in the development and maintenance of a program.
- Regression testing can be applied to system testing, unit testing, or any other sort of testing that is based on a reasonably stable set of test suites.
- The amount of record keeping that regression testing requires necessitates using an automatic mechanism to capture test results, record them in a database, and generate reports.
- Regression testing cannot produce any useful information until there is enough functional code to test.
- Nightly regression testing has an impact on the social dynamics of a group of programmers. Looking at the previous night's regression reports each morning becomes part of their routine. In many cases, the most efficient way to distribute regression reports is by e-mail. However, you can use regression reports to foster communication between programmers. Instead of distributing regression reports by e-mail, post a hard copy on a wall near a spot that you would like to become a gathering place for discussion.

IMPLEMENTATION

The most important type of analysis that you will do with regression-testing data is comparing the results between one test run and the next. A tabular report or matrix is usually the most efficient way to present this information. A graph of the number of failed tests can also be useful.

RELATED PATTERNS

System Testing   Regression testing is commonly used with system testing.

Unit Testing   Regression testing is sometimes used with unit testing.

Acceptance Testing [Grand99]

SYNOPSIS

Acceptance testing is done to ensure that delivered software meets the needs of the customer—the person or organization that contracted for its development. Such testing is usually performed by the customer. Acceptance testing is done according to a plan. The purpose of an acceptance-testing plan is to ensure that the software developers and the customer agree on when the software is complete and ready for its intended use.

CONTEXT

Suppose you are a consultant who is in the business of developing custom software. An orthodontist has approached you about writing some software for his business. This orthodontist has 14 offices in 3 states and has many orthodontists working for him. His business is still expanding. He is convinced that he has outgrown the canned software that he is currently using to run his business.

He has many ideas about the software he wants you to build, including reselling it to other orthodontists. As you listen to the details of what he has in mind, you hear him change his mind about a number of details. You become concerned that he will steadily change what he asks for as the project progresses. He wants the work done for a fixed price. You are concerned that a fixed price will not be adequate, unless he agrees in advance to a firm specification of what will be in the software.

The orthodontist, on the other hand, is nervous about the whole project. He listens to your concerns and wonders if you can really deliver everything he has requested.

You both satisfy your concerns by agreeing that before you receive your final payment, the orthodontist will verify that the software you deliver passes agreed-upon tests. Testing to verify that software meets a customer's specifications is called *acceptance testing* because the customer generally is not required to accept the software until it passes these tests.

FORCES

- Customers want to be sure that they are receiving what they want. They don't want to be stuck with software that is not what they want or that does not meet their needs.
- Software developers want to avoid a situation where the customer is dissatisfied because newly developed custom software does not meet the customer's needs, but those needs were never expressed to the developer.
- If the customer and the developer agree in advance on the procedure that the customer will use to evaluate the delivered software, they can satisfy both concerns. The customer knows that the developer has agreed to be held to a standard with which the customer feels comfortable. The developer knows that the customer has agreed to use only the agreed-upon procedures to evaluate the software and has agreed to not introduce any new issues.
- Procedures for evaluating the software must be objective in nature; otherwise, you will not achieve the goal of deciding in advance how the customer will evaluate the software. Tests such as "the screen must look good" are so subjective that they can be a source of much disagreement. Tests such as verifying that the screens of a program conform to a written guideline are preferable.

SOLUTION

Neither software developers nor their customers want to disagree about whether the software that the developer delivers is what the customer had requested. In order to avoid this, they can agree on an acceptance-testing plan before the developer begins work on the project.

An acceptance-testing plan should include the following elements:

- A statement specifying the scope of the acceptance-testing plan should be included. It should specify the deliverables to be tested, such as software components, operating environment, or hardware. It should also specify high-level goals for acceptance testing. Some typical goals are:

    - The new system must produce results identical to an existing system.
    - The new software must be able to process a certain number of transactions per minute.
    - The new software must perform computations with a minimum level of accuracy.

- A description of the tests to be performed and the environment in which they are to be performed, to the extent that they are known in advance, should be included.
- Test data to be used in acceptance testing should be specified. If possible, the data used for testing should be actual production data to insure a realistic test.
- An acceptance-testing plan is usually written before or at the beginning of a development project. For this reason, many of the details needed to specify the tests to be performed are not known or are not available when the plan is written. This problem is handled in acceptance plans by specifying who will be responsible for developing the necessary detailed test plans, tests, test environments, and technical support. The plan must also specify how the parties involved will agree to these details.
- A statement of who must certify the software as having passed the acceptance test should be included.

The actual tests included in an acceptance-testing plan are determined by what is important to the customer. Any type of test is appropriate, so long as it is objective in nature. Testing aspects of the software such as its functionality or its ability to process a minimum volume of data are appropriate. Even the speed and accuracy with which the customer's employees are able to use the software is appropriate, provided that it is measured in an objective way.

CONSEQUENCES

- Acceptance testing makes it much less likely that a software developer and the developer's customer will argue over whether the developer met the intended functionality of the resulting software.
- People who are responsible for conducting acceptance testing very naturally tend to adopt an attitude of suspicion about the software that they test. Such suspicion can be constructive. However, in combination with unfamiliarity with the software, it can impede the acceptance process.

  There is a natural tendency for people who are working with software that they mistrust and with which they are unfamiliar to assume that if something goes wrong, it is caused by a software fault rather than by their own unfamiliarity with the software. Such experiences can be followed by much unproductive discussion until the actual nature of the problem is determined.

  Something you can do to make acceptance testers more familiar with the software beforehand and help provide them with a realistic level of suspicion is to have some of the acceptance testers observe as the developers conduct their final tests.

- It is possible to spend time debating the details of an acceptance-testing plan. The advantage of spending the time on an acceptance-testing plan is that because it is at the beginning of the process, each party has less invested in the outcome of the debate. This may allow for a calmer and less emotional discussion. It may also allow the parties to discover that they cannot come to an agreement before they have gone to the expense of developing the software.

RELATED PATTERNS

System Testing   System testing is often the final form of testing that a software developer performs on software before turning it over to the customer for acceptance testing.

Clean Room Testing [Grand99]

SYNOPSIS

People who design software should not discuss specifications or their implementation with the people who design tests for that software.

CONTEXT

Jeff and Chuck work for a company that produces electronic postage scales. Whenever any country changes its postage rates, the company must produce memory modules with the new rates for that country's postage scales. Jeff is in charge of the group that maintains the software that is used to program memory modules for the scales. Chuck is in charge of the group that tests the memory modules to ensure that the scales will compute the correct postage in all cases.

Jeff and Chuck prefer to receive information about a change in postage rates in the form of rate tables that specify the amount of postage to be paid for every possible weight in every possible circumstance. Because they need to know about rate changes as early as possible, it is common for them to receive a rate change in whatever form it is written by legislators. Sometimes, legislators authorize rate changes in ways that are subject to interpretation.

One day, Jeff and Chuck have lunch together. They discuss a rate change that they are working on for a South American country. Chuck remarks that the rate seems straightforward, since it simply specifies that all rates are increased by 20 pesos. Jeff reminds Chuck that the country in question has a special rounding rule for amounts over 1000 pesos. Chuck thanks Jeff, and both teams implement the software and test to account for the special rounding rule.

When they ship a prototype scale to that country's postal authorities, they find out that the programming for the new rates and the programs that test the rates are both wrong. After a conversation with that country's postal authorities, Jeff and Chuck determine that the rate change is not subject to the rounding rule after all.

If they had not had that conversation about the rate change, the tests would have been implemented with a different interpretation of the specification and the ambiguity would have been found earlier, saving time and money.

FORCES

- Both the development of software and development of tests for the software are driven by detailed specifications.
- Specifications often contain ambiguities. Sometimes the ambiguities are apparent to people who implement software or tests for the software based on the specifications. In such cases, people may try to resolve the ambiguities before they implement anything based on them.
- Much of software test design is about ensuring that software conforms to the specifications on which it is based.
- When ambiguities in specifications are not apparent to implementers, the ambiguities will be discovered during testing if the people who design tests for software interpret the specifications in a different way than the people who design the software.
- Testing will not detect the ambiguities if test designers and software designers interpret the specifications in the same way.
- When test designers and software designers discuss specifications or the way in which they implement the specifications, the likelihood that they will interpret the specifications in the same way is increased.

SOLUTION

To ensure independent interpretation of specifications by software designers and test designers, the two groups should avoid discussing the specifications, as well as any topics related to the interpretation or implementation of the specifications.

CONSEQUENCES

- Software-development and software-testing groups do not steer each other toward a common interpretation of an ambiguity in a specification.
- Ambiguities in a specification that are not detected before testing are more likely to be found during testing.
- Development and testing groups may duplicate each other's efforts in analyzing a specification.

B I B L I O G R A P H Y

[Aho-et al.86] Alfred V. Aho, Ravi Seti, and Jeffery D. Ullman.
      Compilers, Principles, Techniques and Tools. Reading, Mass.:
      Addison-Wesley, 1986.

[Beck-Cunningham87] Kent Beck and Ward Cunningham.
      "Window per Task."
      http://c2.com/cgi/wiki?WindowPerTask. 1987.

[Beck97] Kent Beck. *Smalltalk Best Practice Patterns.* Upper
      Saddle River, N.J.: Prentice Hall PTR, 1998.

[Brown98] Kyle Brown. "Convert Exceptions."
      http://c2.com/cgi/wiki?ConvertExceptions. 1998.

[Coram-Lee98] Todd Coram and Jim Lee. "Experiences—
      A Pattern Language for User Interface Design."
      http://www.pobox.com/~tcoram/papers/experiences/
      Experiences.html. 1998.

[Duff88] Tom Duff. A Usenet posting reproduced at
      http://www/mindspring.com/~mgrand/duffs-device.html.
      1988.

[Gold97] Russell Gold. "Return New Objects from Accessor Methods." http://c2.com/cgi/wiki?ReturnNewObjectsFromAccessor Methods. 1997.

[Grand99] The present volume.

[Larman98] Craig Larman. *Applying UML and Patterns.* Upper Saddle River, N.J.: Prentice Hall PTR, 1998.

[Meyer92] Bertrand Meyer. "Applying 'Design by Contract.' " *Computer* (IEEE), 25(10): 40–51. October 1992.

[Pryce98] Nat Pryce. "Copy Mutable Parameters." http://c2.com/cgi/wiki?CopyMutableParameters. 1998.

[Schmidt-Harrison96] Douglas C. Schmidt and Tim Harrison. "Double-Checked Locking." Paper presented at the 3d Pattern Languages of Programming conference, Allerton Park, Ill., September 4–6, 1996. http://www.cs.wustl.edu/~schmidt/PLoP-96/DC-Locking.ps.gz. 1996.

[Tidwell98] Jenifer Tidwell. "Interaction Patterns." http://www.mit.edu/~jtidwell/interaction_patterns.html. 1998.

[Trost98] Bill Trost. "Define Constants in Interfaces." http://c2.com/cgi/wiki?DefineConstantsInInterfaces. 1998.

A P P E N D I X

Overview of Patterns in Java

Volume 1

Fundamental Design Patterns

Delegation (When not to use Inheritance) [Grand98]   page 53
Delegation is a way of extending and reusing a class by writing another class with additional functionality that uses instances of the original class to provide the original functionality.

Immutable [Grand98]   page 67
The Immutable pattern increases the robustness of objects that share references to the same object and reduces the overhead of concurrent access to an object. It accomplishes this by not allowing an object's state information to change after it is constructed. The Immutable pattern also avoids the need to synchronize multiple threads of execution that share an object.

325

Interface [Grand98]   page 61

Keep a class that uses data and services provided by instances of other classes independent of those classes by having it access those instances through an interface.

Marker Interface [Grand98]   page 73

The Marker Interface pattern uses interfaces that declare no methods or variables to indicate semantic attributes of a class. It works particularly well with utility classes that must determine something about objects without assuming they are an instance of any particular class.

Proxy   page 79

The Proxy pattern forces method calls to an object to occur indirectly through a proxy object that acts as a surrogate for the other object, delegating method calls to that object. Classes for proxy objects are declared in a way that usually eliminates client object's awareness that they are dealing with a proxy. Proxy is a very general pattern that occurs in many other patterns, but never by itself in its pure form.

Creational Patterns

Abstract Factory [GoF95]   page 99

Given a set of related abstract classes, the Abstract Factory pattern provides a way to create instances of those abstract classes from a matched set of concrete subclasses. The Abstract Factory pattern is useful for allowing a program to work with a variety of complex external entities such as different windowing systems with similar functionality.

Builder [GoF95]   page 107

The Builder pattern allows a client object to construct a complex object by specifying only its type and content. The client is shielded from the details of the object's construction.

Factory Method [GoF95]   page 89

You write a class for reuse with arbitrary data types. You organize this class so that it can instantiate other classes without being dependent on any of the classes it instantiates. The reusable class is able to remain independent of the classes it instantiates by delegating the choice of which class to instantiate to another object and referring to the newly created object through a common interface.

Object Pool [Grand98]   page 135
Manage the reuse of objects for a type of object that is expensive to create or only a limited number of a kind of object can be created.

Prototype [GoF95]   page 117
The Prototype pattern allows an object to create customized objects without knowing their class or any details of how to create them. It works by giving prototypical objects to an object that initiates object creation. The creation initiating object then creates objects by asking the prototypical objects to make copies of themselves.

Singleton [GoF95]   page 127
The Singleton pattern ensures that only one instance of a class is created. All objects that use an instance of that class use the same instance.

Partitioning Patterns

Composite [GoF95]   page 165
The Composite pattern allows you to build complex objects by recursively composing similar objects in a treelike manner. The Composite pattern also allows the objects in the tree to be manipulated in a consistent manner, by requiring all of the objects in the tree to have a common superclass or interface.

Filter [BMRSS96]   page 155
The Filter pattern allows objects that perform different transformations and computations on streams of data and that have compatible interfaces to dynamically connect in order to perform arbitrary operations on streams of data.

Layered Initialization [Grand98]   page 145
When you need multiple implementations of an abstraction, you usually define a class to encapsulate common logic and subclasses to encapsulate different specialized logic. That does not work when common logic must be used to decide which specialized subclass to create. The Layered Initialization pattern solves this problem by encapsulating the common and specialized logic to create an object in unrelated classes.

Structural Patterns

Adapter [GoF95]   page 177
An Adapter class implements an interface known to its clients and provides access to an instance of a class not known to its clients. An adapter object provides the functionality promised by an interface without having to assume what class is being used to implement that interface.

Bridge [GoF95]   page 189
The Bridge pattern is useful when there is a hierarchy of abstractions and a corresponding hierarchy of implementations. Rather than combining the abstractions and implementations into many distinct classes, the Bridge pattern implements the abstractions and implementations as independent classes that can be combined dynamically.

Cache Management [Grand98]   page 251
The Cache Management pattern allows fast access to objects that would otherwise take a long time to access. It involves retaining a copy of objects that are expensive to construct after the immediate need for the object is over. The object may be expensive to construct for any number of reasons, such as requiring a lengthy computation or being fetched from a database.

Decorator [GoF95]   page 243
The Decorator pattern extends the functionality of an object in a way that is transparent to its clients by using an instance of a subclass of the original class that delegates operations to the original object.

Dynamic Linkage [Grand98]   page 225
Allow a program, upon request, to load and use arbitrary classes
that implement a known interface.

Façade [GoF95]   page 205
The Façade pattern simplifies access to a related set of objects by
providing one object that all objects outside the set use to communicate with the set.

Flyweight [GoF95]   page 213
If instances of a class that contain the same information can be
used interchangeably, the Flyweight pattern allows a program to
avoid the expense of multiple instances that contain the same
information by sharing one instance.

Iterator [GoF95]   page 185
The Iterator pattern defines an interface that declares methods
for sequentially accessing the objects in a collection. A class that
accesses a collection only through such an interface remains
independent of the class that implements the interface.

Virtual Proxy [Larman98]   page 235
If an object is expensive to instantiate and may not be needed, it
may be advantageous to postpone its instantiation until the
object is needed. The Virtual Proxy pattern hides the fact that an
object may not yet exist from its clients, by having them access
the object indirectly through a proxy object that implements the
same interface as the object that may not exist. The technique of
delaying the instantiation of an object until it is actually needed
is sometimes called lazy instantiation.

Behavioral Patterns

Chain of Responsibility [GoF95]   page 267
The Chain of Responsibility pattern allows an object to send a
command without knowing what object or objects will receive it.
It accomplishes that by passing the command to a chain of
objects that is typically part of a larger structure. Each object in

the chain may handle the command, pass the command on to the next object in the chain, or do both.

Command [GoF95]   page 277
Encapsulate commands in objects so that you can control their selection, sequencing, queue them, undo them, and otherwise manipulate them.

Little Language/Interpreter [Grand98]   page 289
Suppose that you need to solve many similar problems and you notice that the solutions to these problems can be expressed as different combinations of a small number of elements or operations. The simplest way to express solutions to these problems may be to define a little language. Common types of problems you can solve with little languages are searches of common data structures, creation of complex data structures, and formatting of data.

Mediator [GoF95]   page 315
The Mediator pattern uses an object to coordinate state changes between other objects. Putting the logic in one object to manage state changes of other objects, instead of distributing the logic over the other objects, results in a more cohesive implementation of the logic and decreased coupling between the other objects.

Null Object [Woolf97]   page 365
The Null Object pattern provides an alternative to using `null` to indicate the absence of an object to which to delegate an operation. Using `null` to indicate the absence of such an object requires a test for `null` before each call to the other object's methods. Instead of using `null`, the Null Object pattern uses a reference to an object that doesn't do anything.

Observer [GoF95]   page 347
Allow objects to dynamically register dependencies between objects, so that an object will notify those objects that are dependent on it when its state changes.

Capture a snapshot of an object's state so that the object's state can be restored later. The object that initiates the capture or restoration of the state does not need to know anything about the state information. It needs to know only that the object whose state it is restoring or capturing implements a particular interface.

Encapsulates the states of an object as discrete objects, each belonging to a separate subclass of an abstract state class.

Encapsulates related algorithms in classes that are subclasses of a common superclass. This allows the selection of algorithm to vary by object and also allows it to vary over time.

Write an abstract class that contains only part of the logic needed to accomplish its purpose. Organize the class so that its concrete methods call an abstract method where the missing logic would have appeared. Provide the missing logic in subclass methods that override the abstract methods.

One way to implement an operation that involves objects in a complex structure is to provide logic in each of their classes to support the operation. The Visitor pattern provides an alternative way to implement such operations that avoids complicating the classes of the objects in the structure by putting all of the necessary logic in a separate visitor class. The Visitor pattern also allows the logic to be varied by using different Visitor classes.

Concurrency Patterns

If an object's method is called when the object is not in an appropriate state to execute that method, have the method return without doing anything.

Volume 2

GRASP Patterns

the event source(s) from the objects that actually handle the events.

Creator [Larman98] page 65
Determine which class should create instances of a class based on the relationship between the potential creator classes and the class to be instantiated.

Expert [Larman98] page 59
Assign a responsibility to the class that has the information needed to carry out the responsibility.

Law of Demeter [Larman98] page 77
If two classes have no other reason to be directly aware of each other or to be otherwise coupled, then the two classes should not directly interact. Instead of having a class call the methods of another class that it has no other reason to be coupled with, you should have it call that method indirectly through another class. Insisting on such indirection keeps a design's overall level of coupling down.

Low Coupling/High Cohesion [Larman98] page 53
If you find that a class is so highly coupled or lacking in cohesion as to make a design brittle or difficult to modify, then apply other appropriate GRASP patterns to reassign the class' responsibilities.

Polymorphism [Larman98] page 69
When alternate behaviors are selected based on the type of an object, use a polymorphic method call to select the behavior, rather than using `if` statements to test the type.

Pure Fabrication [Larman98] page 73
Fabricate a class that does not represent a problem domain entity when you assign a responsibility to a class, but assigning it to a class that represents a conceptual model problem domain entity would ruin its low coupling or high cohesion. You resolve this problem by fabricating a class that does not represent an entity in your conceptual model.

GUI Design Patterns

Conversational Text [Grand99]   page 109
Design a GUI to accept commands in the form of textual input.

Direct Manipulation [Grand99]   page 127
Allow users to interact with objects by manipulating the representations of objects presented by a GUI.

Disabled Irrelevant Things [Tidwell98]   page 141
Hide or disable GUI elements that are not relevant in the current context.

Ephemeral Feedback [Grand99]   page 137
Provide feedback to users about the status of their work, without interfering with the natural flow of their work.

Explorable Interface [Coram-Lee98]   page 103
Design user interaction to forgive a user's mistakes by allowing the user to undo actions and go back to previous decision points.

Form [Tidwell98]   page 121
Allow a user to enter structured data into a GUI as discrete pieces of information.

Interaction Style [Coram-Lee98]   page 99
Match the GUI's interaction style to the abilities of its users and the application's requirements. The most common styles of interaction are selection, form, direct manipulation, and conversational text.

Limited Selection Size [Grand99]   page 133
Design the presentation of selection interactions to avoid displaying more than a limited number of choices at a time.

Selection [Grand99]   page 113
Allow users to interact with a GUI by selecting commands and data values from lists.

Step-by-Step Instructions [Tidwell98]   page 149
Lead a user through the steps of a task where the GUI tells the user what to do next, rather than the user telling the GUI what to do next.

Supplementary Window [Grand99]   page 143
Display a window for a user interaction that supplements a parent window's interaction. The purpose of the supplementary window is to collect information for the parent window's interaction, display additional information about the parent window's interaction, or provide a notification about the status of the parent's interaction. The supplementary window is shorter lived than its parent.

Window Per Task [Beck-Cunningham87]   page 95
A GUI should have a separate window for each cohesive task a user must perform. All information required to perform the task should be available from the window. The application provides a way to navigate between windows, allowing the user to coordinate tasks.

Organizational Coding Patterns

Accessor Method Name [Grand99]   page 155
Use names and signatures for accessor methods that are easy to read and conform to the JavaBeans specification.

Anonymous Adapter [Grand99]   page 159
Use anonymous adapter objects to handle events. This simplifies the code and allows code that relates to the same event source to exist in the same part of the source code.

Checked versus Unchecked Exceptions [Grand99]   page 195
As part of its contract with its callers, a method can be expected to throw exceptions under certain circumstances. These exceptions should be checked exceptions. Any exceptions thrown by methods that are outside of its contract, such as exceptions to indicate internal errors or to help with debugging, should be unchecked exceptions.

Client Socket [Grand99]   page 215

You need to write code to manage the server side of a socket-based network connection. The code that you write follows a very consistent pattern that revolves around `Socket` objects. Most uses of the Socket class to implement a client follow a very consistent coding pattern.

Composed Method [Beck97]   page 185

Reorganize methods that are too large to easily understand into smaller methods.

Conditional Compilation [Grand99]   page 191

Control whether a compiler includes statements for debugging in the byte codes it generates or ignores those statements.

Convert Exceptions [Brown98]   page 201

Many programs are organized into layers related to different domains, such as database management and an application domain. In such programs, some classes are part of one domain but have methods that call methods of classes that belong to another domain. Such methods should convert exceptions they do not handle from the other domain to their own domain.

Define Constants in Interfaces [Trost98]   page 171

Avoid having to qualify symbolic constant names with the name of the class that defines them. Define them in an interface so that way, any class that implements the interface can use the symbolic names without any qualification.

Extend Super [Beck97]   page 179

Implement a method that modifies the behavior of a superclass's method by calling the superclass's method.

Intention Revealing Method [Beck97]   page 183

If the intention of a call to a general-purpose method is not obvious, then define a method with a meaningful name to call the general-purpose method.

Server Socket [Grand99]   page 207
You need to write code to manage the server side of a socket-based network connection. The code that you write follows a very consistent pattern that revolves around `ServerSocket` and `Socket` objects.

Switch [Grand99]   page 175
Select a piece of code to execute from multiple alternatives based on an `int` data value by using a `switch` statement.

Symbolic Constant Name [Grand99]   page 165
Use symbolic names for constants. A meaningful name makes the purpose of the constant clear to someone reading the code. Symbolic names can also simplify maintenance.

Code Optimization Patterns

Double Checked Locking [Schmidt-Harrison96]   page 239
A multi-threaded program does not initialize a resource until it actually requires the resource. One thread recognizes that that resource is not yet initialized when another thread has already begun the initialization. Avoid duplicating the initialization effort by coordinating the actions of multiple threads.

Hashed Adapter Objects [Grand99]   page 221
Dispatch a method call to an adapter object associated with an arbitrary object. The arbitrary object is used to find the adapter object in a hash table. The Hashed Adapter Objects pattern is most commonly used when an object must be created from unencapsulated data or when unencapsulated data must be dispatched to an object.

Lazy Initialization [Beck97]   page 233
Delay the creation of an object or other expensive action needed to initialize a variable until it is known that the variable will be used.

Lookup Table [Grand99]   page 249
Save the memory consumed by complex code and the time it
takes to execute by precomputing the results and putting them in
a lookup table.

Loop Unrolling [Grand99]   page 243
Reduce the overhead of a loop's control logic by increasing the
amount of work it does in each iteration, so that it can accomplish the same amount of work in fewer iterations. This pattern
trades memory for speed.

Robustness Coding Patterns

Assertion Testing [Grand99]   page 257
Verify that a method conforms to its contract with its callers by
inserting code to test its preconditions, postconditions, invariants, and data conditions at run time.

Copy Mutable Parameters [Pryce98]   page 279
Objects may be passed to a method or constructor that is used to
determine the state of its associated object. If the passed objects
are mutable, then copies of them should be used to determine the
object's state, rather than the original passed object. That prevents changes to the passed object from also changing the state of
the object associated with the method or constructor.

Guaranteed Cleanup [Grand99]   page 265
Ensure that internal data are in a consistent state if an operation
is unable to execute to its normal completion. Ensure that external resources are consistent state and, if appropriate, are released
after an operation is unable to execute to its normal completion.

Maximize Privacy [Grand99]   page 269
Make members of classes as private as possible.

Return New Objects from Accessor Method [Gold97] page 275
Accessor methods return values or objects that indicate an object's
state. If the objects that an accessor method returns are mutable,

then they should be copies rather than the actual state that determines objects. This prevents changes to the returned object from also changing the state of the accessor method's associated object.

Testing Patterns

Acceptance Testing [Grand99]   page 313
Acceptance testing is testing done to ensure that delivered software meets the needs of the customer—the person or organization that contracted for its development. Such testing is usually performed by the customer that the software was developed for. Acceptance testing is done according to a plan. The purpose of an acceptance-testing plan is to ensure that the software developers and the customer that they develop a software system for agree on when the software is complete and ready for its intended use.

Black Box Testing [Grand99]   page 285
Ensure that software meets requirements by designing tests based solely on requirements. Do not base tests on the manner in which the software is implemented.

Integration Testing [Grand99]   page 297
Test individually developed classes together for the first time.

Regression Testing [Grand99]   page 309
Keep track of the outcomes of testing software testing with a suite of tests over time. This allows you to monitor the completion of coding. It allows you to determine if a change to a program introduced new bugs.

System Testing [Grand99]   page 301
Test a program as a whole entity, in an environment similar to the one in which it is intended to be run in, to ensure that it conforms to its specifications.

Unit Testing [Grand99]   page 293
Test individual classes in isolation from the other classes of the program under development.

White Box Testing [Grand99]   page 289
Design a suite of test cases to exhaustively test software by testing
it in all meaningful situations. The set of meaningful situations is
determined from knowledge of the software's internal structure. A
complete set of tests will exercise all the execution paths through
the software.

About the CD-ROM

The CD-ROM contains the complete source code for all the examples that appear in this book, as well as evaluation copies of some software that you might find useful:

- *CodeWizard for Java* from ParaSoft Corporation is a tool for enforcing rules for coding standards. It comes with a set of coding rules that you can customize. You will need to contact Parasoft for an evaluation password to use CodeWizard.
- *jtest!* from ParaSoft Corporation is a tool for white box testing. It aids in the design of white box tests by analyzing the internal structure of your program. It also manages the running of the white box tests. You will need to contact Parasoft for an evaluation password to use jtest! Call (888) 305-0041, then press 4, or send in the license request to license@parasoft.com, wizard@parasoft.com, or jtest@parasoft.com.

- *AssertMate* from RST Technologies is a preprocessor for managing assertions.
- *Together/ J Whiteboard Edition* from Object International is a platform-independent UML modeler that delivers simultaneous Round-trip engineering for Java.
- *OptimizeIt* from Intuitive Systems is a profiling tool that you can use to determine what parts of a program are taking the most time to execute.

The files for some of the figures in this book are located on the author's Web site at www.mindspring.com/~mgrand in .vsd forms. Check the site for updates to the book as well.

The simplest way to navigate the CD-ROM is to open index.html file with a Web browser. This interface contains links to all the examples and software on the CD-ROM. You may also use File Manager to copy files from the directories on the CD-ROM to your hard drive.

User Assistance and Information

The software accompanying this book is being provided as is without warranty or support of any kind. Should you require basic installation assistance, or if your media is defective, please call our product support number at (212) 850-6194 weekdays between 9 A.M. and 4 P.M. Eastern Standard Time. Or, we can be reached via e-mail at: wprtusw@wiley.com.

To place additional orders or to request information about other Wiley products, please call (800) 879-4539.

You may contact the author through his Web site at www.mindspring.com/~mgrand.

I N D E X